ADVANCE PRAISE

You know you're enjoying the read when you just can't put it down to answer the phone! I never wanted to be through with the book! – TN, SOUTH DAKOTA

The consummate New Yorker reinvented herself into the consummate South Dakotan. I love her stories. They're humorous, engaging, and real. – MF, FLORIDA

The author will resonate with many readers: she writes from a point of view that's not only vulnerable, but endearing and hilarious as well. This book is a must read for anyone seeking the basic creature comforts of home, all the while laughing in the face of the unknown. – VH, KENTUCKY

Truly enjoyed this book. It's light hearted, fun, and easy to read with many laughs. This one will surely please… – CH, NEW YORK

It's inspiring to know that a mid-life woman can create an adventurous new life full of wonder and surprises. The author tells her tale with humor and insight. – JK, CALIFORNIA

A good romp through a comedy of contrasts. – MM, SOUTH DAKOTA

Delightful perception of a totally different world. I'm so impressed with her courage to make this life change. – DF, NEW YORK

I was hooked as soon as I read the first line! – AL, MONTANA

Loved these stories about South Dakota from a city perspective. – KM, SOUTH DAKOTA

A "city gal" with a heart as big as this wide-open country, delivering good laughs to warm the soul. – ML, MONTANA

This book makes every city slicker long for South Dakota! – LC, NEW YORK

Charming, light hearted, clever, easy-to-read witty observations about regional differences. – JS, MARYLAND

This was certainly fun to read! – MB, SOUTH DAKOTA

Hailing from neighboring Wyoming, I laughed my way through this delightful book. I even learned a little something about New York City along the way. – KJ, WYOMING

I was moved by this humorous, yet poignant tale of an independent woman's move from the east coast to the west. – LH, NEW YORK

Loved those one-liners! – JH, SOUTH DAKOTA

Marsha Mittman shares the charm of South Dakota with her readers through funny and witty reflections. – AS, NEW JERSEY

I thoroughly enjoyed the comparisons between NY and SD, and chuckled at the predicaments the author found herself in. As a city girl myself, I loved the picture she painted of her new life. – MC, NEW YORK

YOU KNOW YOU MOVED TO SOUTH DAKOTA FROM NEW YORK CITY WHEN...

Marsha Warren Mittman

Scurfpea Publishing L.L.C.

First edition 2020

Cover artwork by James A. Vande Hey.

Author photograph by Anthony Holguin.

Scurfpea Publishing
P.O. Box 46
Sioux Falls, SD 57101
scurfpeapublishing.com
editor@scurfpeapublishing.com

S. E. H.

Acknowledgments

Chicken Soup for the Soul: Time to Thrive – "Taking Flight"
("Sweetheart")

Your Glasses are on Top of Your Head – "Sweetheart"

Heirlooms from the Dakotas – "Finding Home"
(based on "Sweetheart")

Chicken Soup for the Soul: My Kind (of) America – "South
Dakota Hospitality"

Black Hills Literary Journal – "Taco Tummy," "Tinkerbell,"
"Crazed Tourist"

Granite Island/Amber Sea – fifteen "one–line observations"

*Wyoming Writers Annual National Competition: Non–Fiction
Short Story* – "A City Gal's Wild West Adventures"
("Wildlife," "First Date," "Giddiyap")

Contents

To South Dakota and New York City – two exceedingly different, very special places dear to my heart.

These vignettes celebrate "change," and all the myriad ways it helps a person stretch, learn, grow, thrive, and laugh…

You never know who you really are, who you could become, or what you might accomplish until you step outside your comfort zone.

Vive la différence!

YOU KNOW YOU MOVED TO SOUTH DAKOTA FROM NEW YORK CITY...

...when a sixty year old man brings home a trophy and it's a stuffed deer's head, not a twenty year old wife.

...when subway means a sandwich, not a way to get to work.

...when an "open pit" denotes mining techniques rather than your cost of living.

...when "markets" refer to Saturday morning fresh farm produce instead of the Stock Exchange.

Sweetheart

In my search for a new place to live I'd already, over a period of two to three years, visited various locales in nine different states. Nothing seemed to click. Lovely though they may be, Vermont, New Hampshire, the Carolinas, Florida, New Mexico, Montana and California didn't "speak" to me. Having been widowed young – but with two independent children and parents who were alive and well – I was, literally, a free bird for the first time in my life. But where to fly?

So there I was checking out Denver and Fort Collins, the former too similar (albeit on a smaller scale!) to my home city of New York, and the latter too similar to a New York suburb. Alas, alack, what to do? And where next to go?

For the longest time a friend – who had purchased land for retirement in the Black Hills – had been championing South Dakota. South Dakota? Well, I knew it was "out west somewhere, up there someplace." But *really*, South Dakota?!? *Seriously*??

So I'm still standing there, perplexed, in Denver and I make a snap decision – I'm going to visit Spearfish where my friend owns land. With no car, no maps, no GPS, no AAA triptik, no concept of where Spearfish is in relation to Denver (except that it's "up there"), and absolutely no idea where I'm going, I march myself into a Greyhound bus station and ask if they go to South Dakota.

"Of course," is the answer.

"Spearfish?" I ask hopefully.

"Of course," is the answer.

Elated, I proclaim "Put me on the bus!"

And so the adventure began…

Up through Colorado and Wyoming, the Greyhound ticket attendant neglected to mention a few hours' layover in the dead of night awaiting a bus transfer. The locale – an old bar with tufted red velvet walls and a mirrored ceiling – gave new meaning to the term *lay*over. I certainly got an eyeful of the "wild" west that night! What an experience – I never saw so much activity in my life!

But having survived intact, I was absolutely thrilled with my eventual first views of Spearfish as the bus approached the small town. The area felt so vibrant and the air smelled so fresh. The end of the run, the empty bus – save for this lone traveler from Denver – pulled into a closed Conoco gas station very early on a quiet Sunday morning.

The driver, upon hauling my voluminous valise out of the belly of the bus, looked around at the deserted gas station and said, "No one's here. Who's picking you up?"

"Nobody," I responded.

"Whaddaya mean nobody? Who's coming to get you?"

"No one," I repeated. "I don't know anybody here."

"Whaddaya mean you don't know anyone here? Seriously, who's coming to meet you?"

"No one," for the third time. And as the driver looked at me incredulously I explained I'd come to check the area out without knowing anyone in town.

"But don't worry about me," I was quick to reassure him. "I'll get a taxi."

"Sweetheart," he responded, "there are no taxis here."

"OK, so I'll rent a car."

Eyes rolling, hands on hips now, the driver hits me with "Sweetheart, there are no rental agencies here." And I can just hear his brain registering "*crazy city chick…*"

"Not to worry. It's a small town. I'll walk to the nearest motel and figure it out from there."

"Sweetheart," he says again as his eyes drop to my bare feet in my strappy high-heeled city-style summer sandals standing next to the huge valise, "you're not gonna make it two blocks in *those* shoes with *that* valise and the closest motel is two miles. You SURE you don't know anyone here?"

"Not a soul."

Big sigh, a pause, and then he throws my valise back under the bus. I assume he's going to drive me to the nearest motel but no, he announces "Sweetheart, get back in the bus. I'll take you to a car rental."

I protest, but he insists, and off we go, presumably to the next town to a car rental agency. What I didn't know was that this angel of a man at the end of his long run, finished with work on a beautiful Sunday morning, intended to drive me to Rapid City's airport – an hour away – the only place in South Dakota West River territory where an impetuous crazy city chick could rent a car. And then he had to drive an hour BACK to Spearfish where he lived.

On the way to the airport I sat up front next to the bus' door listening to his stories about South Dakota. "Born and bred. My Dad too. Grandad came over from the old country, bought some land and started farming, and that was that... Got two kids of my own. South Dakota's been home for four generations now."

At the airport, as he once again hauled my valise out of the bus' belly after pointing me in the direction of the rental car locations, I offered him $50.00 for his time and courtesy. And I was shocked – he refused the money...

"Sweetheart," he smiled as he shook my proffered hand, "glad to have been able to help." And off he went...

And my decision was made at that moment. I would move to Spearfish, South Dakota. From the beauty I had seen, the fresh air and good vibes I felt, and the kindness I'd experienced, there seemed to be something very special in the area. Something I'd been searching for but – until now – hadn't found.

I didn't discover until this past year that all my relatives back east – after I moved to Spearfish from ten million people to ten thousand – took bets on how fast I'd return to New York City. One month? Three months? Six? One even bet I'd give it a try for a year...

But it's actually going on twenty years now, and all my relatives back in New York have begun calling me that "crazy country chick."

As for the *real* sweetheart of this story? Well, without a doubt it's the bus driver, who wouldn't let a crazy city chick get stranded...

YOU KNOW YOU MOVED
TO
SOUTH DAKOTA
FROM
NEW YORK CITY...

…when a "gold digger" actually mines for gold and isn't someone looking for a rich spouse.

…when a roll-over refers to your car on an icy road – instead of your corporate investment plan.

…when *flambé* denotes a forest fire, not a Baked Alaska dessert.

…when golf and tennis balls signify hail as often as sports.

Crazed Tourist

Oh my goodness, I'm all alone in this great South Dakota darkness, clutching the steering wheel, peering out over my headlights – definitely set on "bright" – anxiously and intently watching for critters on the road. Seemingly huge mountains are to my right; a massive, ominous looking lake is on my left. I'm inching north to the airport. It's five in the morning and pitch black outside. No moon. I have never in my entire life seen such blackness – there isn't light *anywhere*. I live in New York City – directly on Broadway, the "great white way." Am used to "lights, camera, action" twenty-four/seven.

Where the heck is that turn? Does anyone actually live in this state?? Good Lord, I don't even see any houses. There's just "nothing" all over. Whose idea was it to take the first flight of the day anyway?

I finally make it to Highway 44, where the airport is located, and turn east. The night before the motel hostess had said it would take about forty-five minutes. What she hadn't mentioned was that you need infrared equipment to see the road. I'm running late. I'm starting to sweat.

I suddenly realize I'm on some kind of country road – there are actually corn stalks. I panic – shouldn't a major city's airport be on a main Interstate access?? Where the heck *is* this place? Forty-five minutes have come and gone. Having originally come up from Denver, I haven't a clue as to where I'm going…

I finally see a teensy, weensy sign that says "Rapid City Regional Airport." Faint rays of light are starting to break and way off in the distance, up on a hill, I see a really small lonesome-looking building with a light or two twinkling.

Though the building's architecture looks interesting, surely this can't be the airport…it's so small and looks so uninhabited!

Well, of course, it isn't *the* airport…it's a *regional* airport. Where's the main airport? You see, New York City's John F. Kennedy Airport, with its numerous terminals, hangars, cargo facilities, and runways is probably larger than the whole of Rapid City itself. And on the East Coast, regional facilities (i.e. hangars for private planes or commuter flights to nearby destinations) are often located adjacent to a main airport so radar equipment can be shared.

So I pass by Rapid City's Regional Airport and continue on down what I think is Highway 44, anxiously scanning the horizon for the *real* airport. My flight's leaving in thirty minutes and I still have to drop the rental car. HOW am I going to do this? Total panic is setting in – if I miss my flight, the ticket is non-refundable…

Way off in the distance, like the proverbial sentinel on the prairie, I spy a lone radar tower. It's a BIG radar tower – this *has* to be the place. Finally! Maybe I can just make this flight after all! I floor the accelerator, careen towards the tower…make a screeching right turn…and hurtle towards the parking kiosk.

Except it isn't a parking kiosk.

Suddenly two uniformed guards come out of nowhere and point machine guns at me; then two police cars come charging up and screech to a stop directly in front of me, blocking my path. More guns – big guns – point my way. I jam the brakes on, and as the guns advance it slowly dawns on me: what I thought was a "parking kiosk" is some military checkpoint. Did I just plow headlong into Ellsworth Air Force Base, home of the B1 Bomber?

Now as I mentioned, I come from New York City, known for its "Saturday Night Special" revolvers. But never in my life have I had a weapon pointed in my face. Driver's license, additional identification, car rental papers, airplane ticket, a search of the auto, a call to the airline desk – these guys meant business. They certainly weren't taking my story on my say-so.

I guess my mounting hysteria and the proffered airline ticket finally convinced them though, because suddenly one of the guards hopped into one of the military police cars yelling "Follow me!" and drove off back down the road from whence I'd just come.

So there I was, now going west with a military police escort, flying along at 85mph. He led me directly to the Rapid City Regional Airport's departure area – but I still had to drop the rental car. He yelled at me to just leave it with my rental agreement on the front seat (try doing THAT in New York!!), to run for the plane, and not to worry – and that's what I did. I grabbed my suitcase and ran…

I couldn't believe I made the flight – I was thirty minutes late. As I settled in I overheard the flight attendant announce that we'd arrive at our destination on time even though the plane's departure had been delayed so someone could make the flight. I was shocked – could the plane really have been held for ME??

I looked out my window as we took off – the sun had finally broken through and there was a gorgeous sunrise. Down below, however, I noticed that my military escort had hung around. I think he was making sure a certain crazed tourist had definitively left town.

Poor man…little did he know…I'd decided to move to South Dakota!!

YOU KNOW YOU MOVED
TO
SOUTH DAKOTA
FROM
NEW YORK CITY...

…when discussions of "canning" deal with tomatoes and cukes, not getting fired.

…when "passing the buck" has nothing to do with taking responsibility and everything to do with waiting for a better shot.

…when an "open door policy" is how you leave your house, not something reviewed at the United Nations.

South Dakota Hospitality

After my initial visit to South Dakota, when I'd decided to move to the western part of the state, I planned a return trip. I'd only spent time in Spearfish and Rapid City, both of which I thoroughly enjoyed. But were there other areas worth considering?

Besides, there were still lots of interesting tourist sights to check out.

I decided on a swing through the southwestern part of the state, and started making plans for the last two weeks of July. Wow, motel reservations sure were hard to come by in some places, and a few prices were surprisingly high compared to my previous spring visit. South Dakota sure was popular as a tourist destination in the summertime!

And so I left the sweltering, humid heat of a New York City summer. As soon as I exited the Rapid City airport the magnificent views of the distant mountains soothed my soul. I also, amazingly, found my body reacted beneficially to the dry weather. Yup, this was definitely the place for me… As a matter of fact, in case I decided to stay for a longer span of time this visit, I specifically left my New York City return date open.

Scratch one off my bucket list – I finally got to see Mount Rushmore! Scratch another off the list – the monumental mountain carving of Chief Crazy Horse. And then I embarked upon a carefree, lovely, meandering, circular drive further south that took me through a number of South Dakota's famed westernmost Black Hills sites and towns.

I'd stayed a couple days longer than expected, and as time progressed suddenly found it difficult to extend my motel reservations. And then, my last night before departure, I simply couldn't find a room *anywhere*. I'd never run into anything like this before. I've been fortunate, for work, to travel the world and I'd *always* been able to secure a reservation *somewhere*. Even in the most remote of places. But there didn't appear to be a single available room in the entire western half of the state! What the heck?? I called motels, hotels, inns, BnB's – nothing! I had a very early morning flight – and here I was trying to book accommodations over an hour away.

Ridiculous! What in the world was going on?

Turned down on the phone yet again by a BnB owner over a good hour's distance to the airport, eminently frustrated, I finally asked "Is there a convention or something in town tomorrow? Because all rooms everywhere seem to be taken."

His matter-of-fact answer: "Honey, it's Rally." As if I should have just realized it.

Pregnant pause...

Me: "It's what?"

Him: "The Rally. It's Rally time. Don't tell me ya never heard of it. What rock you been hidin' under all ya life? Beginning August is always Rally time. You're not gonna find a room within four hours of Sturgis this time of year."

Me: "Sturgis? That's near Spearfish, isn't it?"

Him, losing patience: "Yeah, that's near Spearfish. Sturgis is Rally headquarters."

Me, totally stupefied: "What's this Rally?"

Him, dumbfounded: "Lady, *where* are you from? You don't know about the Sturgis Rally??"

Me: "Haven't a clue. What are people rallying *for*? Is something political going on?"

There was an audible groan over the phone. "It's not a *political* rally, lady. It's a *motorcycle* rally – the largest in the world! A couple hundred thousand of 'em."

Well, that would certainly explain why I couldn't find a room...

And then I mentioned how I hailed from New York City,

was planning to move to South Dakota, had been checking out the area, and now would probably have to sleep in my car at the airport the night before my flight. I asked if by any chance he knew anyone at all who had a room available…

…and it was his turn to pause.

"Look," he said, "you have to understand you're not goin' to find a room anywhere. These dates are booked up a year ahead, from Rally to Rally. And by the way, that's why prices are higher – this is prime time.

"But since you're gonna be a neighbor, so to speak," he continued, "I can offer you some South Dakota hospitality. Won't be fancy, because I'm completely full, running my tail off."

"Anything, please. I'll take anything at this point."

"OK. My son is bunking with a friend over in Sturgis. You're welcome to use his room. I have no idea what condition he left it in. I'm not even goin' to charge ya for it – I don't have time to clean it up. But at least you'll have a bed – ya won't have to sleep in your car. The airport is crazy now with everyone arriving and all the motorcycles being trucked in for pickup.

"Whenever you get here just drive up to the main house and go inside – the door's unlocked. My son's bedroom is up on the second floor. It's the first door on the right. The bathroom's down the hall – take a towel from the linen closet. And whatever ya do, be careful driving here. There'll be motorcycles swarming all over the place."

And so I spent the eve of my first world-famous Sturgis Motorcycle Rally in the empty dormered bedroom of an eight year old boy, rumpled Superman sheets and all. With playthings scattered all over the floor protected by superhero figures lined up along a windowsill. With a blue and yellow wallpapered wall depicting our solar system, and Little League trophies on a couple shelves. With an orange plastic basketball hoop dangling from the ceiling.

Sometime during the night there was a bit of apprehension: I was awakened by the bedroom door being nudged open. But then a huge furry dog bounded onto the bed to snuggle…

When I left at 5am to make my early flight, the house was silent. I hadn't seen a soul since I arrived the night before. The bikers had been out partying then, and were fast asleep now. I put fifty dollars as a thank you on a kitchen counter with a note – in case my move wasn't yet finalized, I asked for reservations for the following year.

Well now, I *really* did have to see just what this huge Rally was all about…

…and thank my anonymous benefactor, his son, and their big furry dog – in person – for all their very kind hospitality.

This story is from Chicken Soup for the Soul: My Kind (of) America, *copyright © 2017 Chicken Soup for the Soul, LLC. All rights reserved.*

YOU KNOW YOU MOVED TO SOUTH DAKOTA FROM NEW YORK CITY...

…when a fence surrounds your garden and isn't someone selling stolen goods.

…when getting "a good deal" refers to Deadwood rather than a successful business proposition.

…when BBQ means it's branding time, not dinner time.

…when a "fir" means a tree instead of some warm, fuzzy coat.

Learning Curve

It was my first marketing trip in my adopted state of South Dakota. I was so surprised at the differences in foods stocked from those on supermarket shelves back in my home state of New York. Easterners and westerners certainly had dissimilar tastes! Heck, we even called where we shopped by different names: my former supermarket was South Dakota's grocery store!

First, out here in the West it seemed as if nobody liked pretzels. Stores had miles of potato and corn chips, but no pretzels at all. Hellman's mayonnaise was non-existent until I finally discovered it was marketed under a different name in the West. Most cuts of meat looked strange, and it was likely no one ever ate fish. Fresh fish? Forget it… But there sure were loads of bacon and sausage choices. And ribs…

Then there was a curious looking glutinous green concoction in a big bowl at the deli counter next to an equally questionable white creamy glob – I'd never seen either before. And when I asked about a can of cranberry sauce I got "Sorry, hon, only at Thanksgiving." But donuts? Well, donuts were everywhere…

Salsa was also all over… Ditto guacamole… Ditto cheese… Every hot soup near the deli counter had cheese in it: your choice – broccoli cheese, potato cheese, bacon and cheese. And the fresh produce section seemed to be located in a "rain forest" – water spouts continuously and copiously sprinkled veggies to keep them from withering in South Dakota's dry climate. Scallions hereabout were called green onions; fennel was anise.

This was heartland ranching "meat and potatoes" territory,

so compared to New York City there was a fairly limited selection of fruits and veggies. Even so, as a former vegetarian, whatever was in my shopping cart posed a real challenge for the young cashier when it came time to check out. Rutabagas, parsnip, jicama, bok choy, fresh ginger – I unwittingly gave this poor girl a headache…

And so it came time for my groceries to be bagged. A tall, nice-looking older gent – probably working part-time to augment Social Security payments – moved over to my aisle to assist. As the checker once more became engrossed at her register, this gentleman nimbly leaned towards me, over the piles of food, and quietly asked "Can I sack your pop?"

Completely taken aback, I stared at him – the comment just didn't register.

Very serious, he asked again, looking directly into my eyes, "Can I sack your pop?"

Now I'm a mature, experienced, somewhat attractive woman, and have had my fair share of male attention. Occasionally unwanted attention. Totally confused and incredulous, I thought to myself, "Good Lord, WHAT is this man talking about? Men must certainly be aggressive out this way. I've only been a South Dakota resident for one day – can this possibly be a proposition?? Using some kind of colloquialism or slang? Is this man "hitting" on me? In the supermarket yet? *What* is this man asking me?"

He started to ask a third time and I guess, seeing my wide-eyed shell-shocked reaction, closed his mouth, made an executive decision, and reaching right past me for my cans of soda, he proceeded to place them in a bag…

"Sack my pop?!? Aha! My soda cans got bagged…"

Clearly there's a learning curve I'm gonna have to master out this way…

YOU KNOW YOU MOVED TO SOUTH DAKOTA FROM NEW YORK CITY...

…when a "great rack" compliments a deer's antlers, not a woman's chest.

…when a Hog refers to a Harley instead of someone seriously overeating.

…when "rally" connotes Sturgis rather than a stock market surge.

…when you change clothes four times in ten minutes and it's not for a runway fashion show, it's because of the weather.

Giddiyap

"C'mon Mom, you just can't live out west without riding a horse!!"

This was the harangue I got, every phone call, prior to my New York City-based daughter's first trip to my new home – I'd moved to South Dakota after my husband passed away. After a Mount Rushmore visit, horseback riding was next on her bucket list. The closest she'd ever come to riding was watching people astride on the trails in New York City's Central Park – for which the price was absolutely outrageous. So as far as she was concerned, it was now or never out here in South Dakota.

I'd never been on a horse and was truly loathe to try it. I'd actually loved pony rides as a child in a local park every Sunday. I remember those treks fondly – going round and round a little corral; feeding my favorite black and white pony a carrot each week; patiently standing and awaiting my turn.

My trepidation to get on an actual full-grown steed stemmed from my late husband. Over the years, while on vacations, we'd had ample opportunities and I recall asking him to join me. But he was adamant – no riding for either of us. He'd had a friend who in his late teens went horseback riding. The horse spooked; the friend was thrown. He cracked his head on a boulder, there was a serious injury to his neck, and the friend was never "the same" thereafter. For my husband, that translated into "no horses."

But my husband was gone now and here was my daughter throwing my own words back at me: "You're always telling me to try new things, to stretch myself, to not have fear. So, what about YOU? Don't the same rules apply to you?"

I finally acquiesced, but told her she was in charge. This was something I wasn't organizing. If she really wanted to go riding she had to do the research to plan the outing herself.

Of course she did…

So there we were, somewhere down in the southern Black Hills, at a ranch that advertised trail rides. Seven other people were milling about, waiting, like us, to be matched to horses for a four-hour jaunt. Good Lord, FOUR hours?!? What the heck do you do on a horse for FOUR solid hours??

One by one, people were saddling up. My turn came – I mentioned to the handler that this was my initial foray and I was really nervous. He told me not to worry, that he'd chosen a really gentle horse for me, a horse that knew just what to do. When I asked for some instructions, simple things like making the horse stop or nudging it to go forward, or even how to hold the reins, I was told there was no need. "The horse knows where to go and what to do."

Ohhhh-kaaaay. I'm really not too happy about this, but them's the rules and everyone is chafing at the bit – horses and people alike – to get going. Far be it for me to make a fuss…

And then he brought my horse over to me. This horse was HUGE. Everyone else – including a ten/twelve year old – was able to stick their left foot in a stirrup, haul themselves up, and swing their right leg over to get mounted. I'm fairly short, but an adult, and yet I couldn't even get my foot high enough to place it into the stirrup! As I started to protest, the handler shushed me and brought over a portable step thingamajig to climb up so I could get atop the horse's back. Mission accomplished…

But once up there I suddenly realized I was VERY VERY far from the ground!!

The handler proceeded to line us up in single file. My daughter and I were at the end, after the seven other riders. I was number eight; my daughter brought up the rear. The handler was up front – seemingly way far away. Another thing not to be happy about!

And so the entourage departed amidst much laughter and

shouting and picture taking. Coupled with my white knuckled fists clutching the reins…

All actually went well initially. I didn't quite understand why every so often my horse kept pulling his head left out of line, and then right, out of line again. No one else's horse up ahead seemed to be behaving similarly. But hey, the day was lovely, the trail was pretty, my daughter was living her dream – and if I didn't look down I could almost imagine I was taking a little stroll through the woods.

This went on for quite a while, and lulled by the horse's slow, rocking motion, I was actually beginning to relax a bit. And then, suddenly, my horse really pulled to the left. I yanked on the reins to try and get it back into line, but the horse just kept pulling against them. I yelled to the handler, but he was too far ahead to hear me. My daughter, behind me, asked what I was doing to make the horse pull left but I assured her it was the horse's inclination, not mine.

So there we were, with all the horses – though spread out – still neatly lined up in a row. Except for my guy, still at number eight, who was prancing along three feet to the left of everyone else.

And then, of course as we were traversing a rocky sloping incline – probably part of a dry stream – my horse just took off. Started galloping dead ahead, down the tumbling rolling stones, like a bat outta hell. And I could hear my daughter's panicked waning voice, "Mom, what in the world are you doing??"

At that point all I was doing, literally, was holding on for dear life.

And screaming…

One by one my horse passed all the others. Left them in the dust, as we say out here in the West. He finally got to the front of the line, slowed down, and positioned himself directly in front of the handler. Who calmly looked at frazzled me and said, "I told you he knows what to do. He's usually a lead horse and I guess he wasn't too happy way back there in the lineup."

So OK, I finally went horseback riding.

I sincerely think a merry-go-round is more my speed…

YOU KNOW YOU MOVED TO SOUTH DAKOTA FROM NEW YORK CITY...

... when the stars you see at night are named Hercules and Perseus instead of Pitt and Clooney.

...when "the season" signifies hunting rather than debutante balls.

... when a "brand" distinguishes your cattle, not your clothes.

...when global warming experts are more concerned with the rear of a cow than the rear of an auto.

Mystery

After deciding to move, I initially commuted back and forth between New York City and Spearfish, SD for a few years. I occasionally took a shuttle from Rapid City's airport to my home, fifty or so miles distant. The service was advertised as a "shared" ride. Certainly more local destinations had multiple passengers, but I was usually the sole client on my Spearfish runs.

So it was surprising late one evening, when there I was, ready and raring to get home, luggage all corralled, and the driver said we had to wait. I'd have company on this ride.

He then proceeded to disappear – I assumed to look for the missing wayward traveler. I stood there in the airport, scanning the scattering passengers, wondering why my tripmate was taking so long.

Nobody materialized. About twenty minutes passed. The airport was becoming deserted – we'd been the last flight of the night. I began to wonder if even the shuttle driver had forgotten me.

And then I saw him, hurrying my way, carrying a red plastic case about eighteen inches square.

"OK," he said, "let's load up. Ready to go…"

"Where's the second passenger?" I asked.

"Right here," he said, holding up the red case.

As we approached the van he indicated I should sit in the back. While climbing in, I noticed he very carefully placed the mysterious red case on the front passenger seat, and carefully strapped it into place – then loaded my luggage into the rear.

"Well, this is certainly novel," I mused as we took off.

Shared rides aren't popular in New York City where thousands of taxi cabs troll the streets at any given time. The only two occasions I'd ever experienced sharing was during a massive snowstorm when subways and buses stopped running, and when a huge electrical outage hit. Yes, there were some shared vans to local airports but, generally, there were so many traffic delays in town people hated the idea of more time wasted picking up additional passengers. Better to go it alone – if not with a taxi, there was always a bus, Uber, or train available.

Out on Long Island, where I originally lived with my husband and children, it was a different story. Few taxis were available. So when the Long Island Railroad pulled into local stations from New York City, the couple taxis on hand loaded as many riders as possible into each vehicle, to dispatch to a specific area. If your destination happened to be the furthest point, sometimes the drive to your house could take as long as the train ride from the city!

With these lengthy Long Island runs in mind, I wondered whether the strange red box's drop would occur before or after I reached home. And how long the delivery would take if the former.

I also wondered what precious cargo the mysterious red box held – the driver was certainly handling it with extreme care, checking it every few minutes as he drove. It seemed to be a refrigerated case. Could it, I considered, hold a body part for an organ transplant?

Nah, then it would have been dropped at the hospital in Rapid City. There was no other major medical facility further west in the state. My curiosity was piqued, but the driver just wasn't a chatty guy.

Finally, about half way home he mentioned we'd be stopping in Sturgis, just off the Interstate; that he wouldn't be too long, he just had to drop the red case. And so, holding my breath, I waited for the outcome of the mystery.

He pulled off the Interstate; navigated some dark, barren local streets; and then drove into the parking lot of a veterinarian's office. I was dumbfounded. Could there be a small ailing animal or bird within the case, waiting for medical aid? Was a team waiting to do surgery?

He very carefully unstrapped the case, and carrying it, approached the building. Its door opened immediately; someone had actually been standing there, waiting for him.

After we were back on the road, still silent, unable to contain myself any longer, I finally blurted out "*What* was in that case? Had to have been pretty crucial for someone to have been anxiously waiting at the door so close to midnight!"

The driver casually turned to me and said "Bull semen."

Pause.

"Excuse me?" the city gal squeaked.

"Bull semen," he repeated. "'AI,' artificial insemination appointments start early tomorrow morning. There was a shortage. The vet bought some from another rancher, but the order came in late. Let me tell you, this drop was reeeeally important." And then he lapsed into silence once more and continued driving.

Well, they say Manhattan has everything, but "gotcha" NYC – bet bull semen can't be found in the Big Apple!

Hah! I'm gonna email all my friends back east and tell them my shuttle co-passenger was SD's prime stud!

…they just better not ask me what he looked like…

YOU KNOW YOU MOVED
TO
SOUTH DAKOTA
FROM
NEW YORK CITY...

…when something goes "bump in the night" and it's a deer on I90, not a burglar.

…when you realize there actually IS something called a range and it isn't your stove.

…when "getting rattled" means hearing a snake rather than being stressed.

…when everyone comes to visit in August because of the hot action, instead of leaving town because of the heat.

Taco Tummy

So there I am, about 11pm, flying down I90 towards Spearfish, SD. My stomach is loudly complaining after its first-ever introduction to a taco salad at Rapid City's Home Show. New to the area, I vaguely remember a "24 hour" supermarket. I decide to exit at Jackson – not my usual egress – and head over to the store for Alka-Seltzer.

Once I exit, I notice in my rear-view mirror, a large white van with a revolving blue light atop its roof. I recall a hospital near the supermarket and figure that's the vehicle's destination – that it's an ambulance sans siren since it's late at night. And I'm guessing it's not much of an emergency since it's following me instead of rushing ahead.

All of a sudden I hear a huge voice blaring out of a megaphone, demanding "Black car, pull over."

"That can't be me," I think, as I try to remember the color of my rental car. And anyway, why would an ambulance want someone to pull over when there's an empty adjacent lane?"

The megaphone voice gets louder and more insistent: "BLACK. CAR. PULL. OVER."

My stomach is growling, my head is starting to pound, and just as I'm considering pulling over to let this ridiculous vehicle pass me – maybe my rental auto IS black – two police cars come flying out of a cross street, left and right, to block my way. Two officers jump out of the vehicles, and yes, two rifles are now pointed at me.

"Oh good grief," I sigh, "here we go again." Déjà vu, shades of the Ellsworth Air Force Base fiasco!! HOW do I get myself into these situations??

I stop. The driver of the ambulance behind me jumps out; approaches with gun drawn; orders me out of the car.

I don't get out. I come from New York where there are ploys like this all the time. I have no idea who this man is; he's not in uniform; I don't understand why two police cars are blocking my way; it's close to midnight; streets are deserted. I also feel like I'm going to barf – and now THIS!! God, this really IS the *Wild* West!

I tell the ambulance driver I don't understand what's happening – I'm going to phone the local police station. He looks at me incredulously.

"Lady, I AM the police. I called for backup when you resisted arrest – that's why the two police cars are up ahead. Get out of the car NOW."

It finally dawns on me, in between stomach cramps, that just maybe I don't quite have a handle on this situation…

"Wait – I was resisting arrest?"

"Yes, didn't you see the flashing lights? And, if you reach into your purse – you say 'for your phone' but it could be for a weapon – I will shoot."

"I didn't know you were police – I thought your van was an ambulance en route to the hospital here. Listen, where I come from law enforcement vehicles have the word "POLICE" written backwards above their windshields. That way drivers looking into rear-view mirrors realize police vehicles are behind them. I would've stopped had I known.

"But what was I doing wrong?"

"You were driving thirty-five in a twenty-five mile per hour zone, and then resisted arrest when I tried to stop you."

"I never saw a speed limit sign when I exited so figured 35mph would be reasonable."

"Well, it's twenty-five and the sign is right there on the pole with all the organizations here in town."

"You mean that skinny pole with the Masons, Lions, and everyone's cousins? I never even saw the speed sign!

"Look, I just came from the Home Show in Rapid City. I

own land here. I'm going to be your neighbor. I'm headed over to the supermarket because I have a terrible stomach-ache – I really need some Alka-Seltzer. Can't we just chalk this up to the misunderstanding it is?"

"Who'd you buy your land from?" he barks. I tell him. He nods his head. I also give him the name of the builder I conferred with at the Home Show. Nods his head again. Hope springs eternal I just might extricate myself from this mess unscathed.

"Where're you staying?" I mention my motel, and its manager's name.

I repeat I really feel sick and need to get to the supermarket.

He finally waves the two police cars off and agrees I was confused about his vehicle, so doesn't cite me for resisting arrest. But dang, he still gives me a speeding ticket.

I cringe.

Then he asks if I know where the supermarket is located. When I mention I just have a vague idea he smiles at his captive and says "Follow me."

So there I am with my *second* South Dakota police escort!

I follow him to the supermarket – at 25mph of course. He waits while I purchase my Alka-Seltzer. And, naturally, tails me all the way back to my motel. Back in my room I take not only two Alka-Seltzer for my stomach, but two aspirin for my spinning head…

A couple weeks later I notice, when exiting once more onto Jackson from I90, that the small speed limit sign has been pulled from the line-up of organizations and now stands by its lonesome on a little post all its own, impossible to miss.

So I wonder – did my fine pay for the new post?

YOU KNOW YOU MOVED TO SOUTH DAKOTA FROM NEW YORK CITY...

…when mending fences means a cow took a stroll – not making up with your mother-in-law.

.

…when bareback signifies no saddle rather than the latest Oscar de la Renta fashion.

…when you realize blinds aren't always window treatments – they're also protective enclosures for cattle.

Great Places / Famous Faces

My New York City-based high-tech son had arrived for his first visit to South Dakota. I'd been extolling the beauty of the area for months now, and so we immediately set out on a sightseeing tour.

Spearfish was home. So naturally, after driving him through some local sites, we embarked on a drive through Spearfish Canyon, a Designated Scenic Byway.

My son, who'd always loved animals – but had never been able to own one for various reasons – was absolutely delighted with sightings of deer, wild turkeys, a mama raccoon with three raggle-taggle babies, and the Canyon's famed huge, old, impressively horned all-white mountain goat. He couldn't believe he'd seen so much wildlife in one short drive.

"Just wait until tomorrow," I promised him, "when we go south. There's more to come – buffalo and 'begging burros' to begin with. Maybe we'll even see an eagle. And then we'll top everything off with a trip to Mount Rushmore."

The following day didn't disappoint: the majestic buffalo were roaming. To my son's absolute delight the burros stuck their heads through our open car windows looking for food. We saw groupings of mountain goats and herds of antelope, and not one, but two eagles. Then we were off to the pride of South Dakota, Mount Rushmore…

Standing and gazing up at the four impressive U.S. presidents' heads carved into the imposing mountaintop, my son marveled, "Well, the animals were really great. But nowhere else can you see such instantly recognizable, iconic faces that symbolize contributions to mankind."

His comment struck a chord and resurrected an amusing, typical "New York moment…"

Back in Manhattan, I'd gone to the theater one evening. When the play was over I planned to meet a friend for a late dinner at a well-known, highly recommended, lovely restaurant located directly in the Theater District in an area known as "Restaurant Row."

Upon entering the elegant old brownstone building in which the restaurant was located, a maitre'd asked me to please follow him past the bar area to the dining room beyond, where my table was reserved. I proceeded to do so.

But then I stopped dead in my tracks. Sitting there, right in front of me, having one grand 'ole time at the bar laughing and joking around, were three instantly recognizable iconic faces – faces that made contributions, in their own way, to humanity through their artistic and charitable endeavors: actors Robert DeNiro and Jack Nicholson, and singer Tony Bennett. All together…

New Yorkers, and visitors to the city, love to play "star spotting." Occasionally one gets lucky and fleetingly catches a famous face ducking into or out of an appointment somewhere. But to see three such legends at one time – just sitting, relaxing, and laughing?

Rarely happens.

"Why so quiet?" my son suddenly asked while still gazing at Washington, Jefferson, Roosevelt, and Lincoln. And so I related my other encounter with iconic male faces…

"No way…" my son commented.

"Absolutely true," I answered. "You know I wouldn't tell a lie."

And I swear, as the words passed my lips, George shot me a wink…

YOU KNOW YOU MOVED TO SOUTH DAKOTA FROM NEW YORK CITY...

…when "take a hike" doesn't mean you're not wanted.

…when "game management" deals with elk, deer, and antelope rather than directing traffic at a World Series play-off.

…when "milking" connotes cows, not squeezing a client for a good business deal.

…when "stalks" have to do with gardens, instead of celebrity-obsessed groupies.

First Date

I was attending my first concert in the Black Hills since moving to the area. Hearing my New York accent when I thanked her for assisting me, the curious hostess who guided me to my single seat proceeded to ask a few questions. We chatted for a couple minutes standing there in the aisle to the left of the row in which my seat was located. It was when I mentioned I was widowed that a man sitting in the row directly in front of mine, second seat in, turned around to check me out – he'd evidently been doing a bit of eavesdropping!

When I ultimately took my seat – surprise – it was located directly behind this gent! Who proceeded to turn around again, introduce himself, and chat me up until the concert started…

Intermission, and he again initiated a conversation. So I checked HIM out. Surely seemed personable enough, fairly nice looking in a weathered sort of way, dressed in a casual pair of pants and sweater as is the norm hereabouts.

On my way to the Ladies Room before the concert started again, the hostess caught up with me and said "I see Hugh is monopolizing you. He's a well-known figure here in the Hills."

And so, when "well-known figure in the Hills Hugh" asked for my phone number at the end of the concert, with the hostess' evident mark of approval, I handed it over.

Didn't take more than a couple days for Hugh to call. He suggested dinner in Deadwood at his favorite buffet. I was thrilled as I'd previously only driven through the town without stopping for food or to walk around and savor its Old West flavor. Hugh said he'd show me the sights.

I was staying in a Spearfish motel at the time, while planning to build a permanent place to live. Since Hugh was picking me up directly from work and wasn't exactly sure when he'd leave, I told him to have the motel's front desk attendant ring my room when he arrived. Then I'd come down to the lobby to meet him…

Like a teenager on her first date, I agonized over what to wear. This, after all, was my first date in my adopted state. And I found that having worked in New York City all my adult life, having an apartment directly in Manhattan for the past half dozen years, and having lived in close proximity to the "Big Apple" ever since birth, I was constantly "over-dressing" out here in the West. I hadn't quite yet picked up on that casual sensitivity and sensibility that reigns supreme in the area. Especially since I'd been an Interior Designer – where everything matched, was perfect, and was "just so." I couldn't quite get the hang of the fact that wedding attire in the West sometimes simply meant a silk – instead of cotton – blouse thrown over the same 'ole, same 'ole pair of blue jeans!

But I finally got my act somewhat together and waited for Hugh's call. When it came, I sauntered into the lobby to meet him…

…and couldn't find him! There were a half dozen people milling around in the lobby but absolutely no one I could recall! I stood there hesitating, then heard "Marsha…," and couldn't believe my eyes. There, I swear, walking towards me, was Indiana Jones – Harrison Ford in the movie "Raiders of the Lost Ark." The apparition was decked out, head to toe, in a worn, beaten, wide-brimmed tan leather hat with a braided band into which an assortment of feathers had been tucked (one particularly long at about eighteen inches); an ancient, stained, camel-colored suede jacket with long, decaying, droopy fringes hanging from the chest, both arms, and its hemline; old, cracked, leather gloves; and some kind of brown jodhpurs with leather sides tucked into knee high water-proof-looking light green boots sporting caked, dried mud.

I wasn't exactly expecting "well-known figure in the Hills Hugh" to show up in a suit. I'd already been warned by a local that if I saw any male wearing a suit in the area it meant someone had died and I was looking at the town's undertaker. But *really*, Indiana Jones???

The impression got more bizarre when I climbed into his pickup – it was littered with a dozen or so rifles and a mean-looking eight to ten foot long whip.

Uh-oh… Good Lord, what had I let myself in for?

I kept consoling myself with the fact that the hostess at the concert had said Hugh was a well-known local. But when he turned off the main route to Deadwood and proceeded to drive through an isolated back canyon's dirt road, I sure as heck started getting a little nervous. I kept glancing at the guns and the whip – had the hostess misjudged him?

To boot, he didn't answer any of my questions. I was trying to make casual conversation, but it all seemed one-sided and my queries were really ignored. Dusk was starting to fall; I was starting to worry…

Finally, after a few silent, tense minutes, way off in the distance I saw a couple twinkling lights up on some hills I knew to be Deadwood. Big sigh of relief… Then Hugh turned to me and said "I told ya I'd show ya some sights, so I took back roads to show ya the canyon. We'll talk over dinner. I'm deaf in my right ear, so can't make out anything you been sayin'…"

Over dinner, Hugh made sure I sat on his left so we could have a normal conversation. Turns out, yes, he'd just come from work and he was a private for-hire hunting guide for pheasant – for which South Dakota is famous. Hence the get-up and water-proof boots. Supplies his clients with everything – even the guns, hence the dozen rifles in his car. Was deaf in his right ear from all the years of hearing his gun's shots. And the whip? Well, he always carries that around his waist in case of mountain lions or rattle-snakes. See – he really was Indiana Jones!

Alas, alack, it was mutually evident – though ultimately

a pleasant evening, I was too citified for him and he too rusticated for me. And so, unlike Harrison Ford's escapades, there was to be no "sequel" to this particular Indiana Jones adventure.

But just for a moment there it sure had all the makings of a great flick: eccentric characters, a bit of mystery, strange dialogue, some weird elements, beautiful scenery – and of course, one great evocative signature outfit worthy of an Oscar for costume design…

YOU KNOW YOU MOVED TO SOUTH DAKOTA FROM NEW YORK CITY...

...when "crops" mean corn, sunflowers, and soybeans, rather than women's cut-off summer pants.

...when scoping out a hot target means a deer, not a dame.

...when "getting the dirt on someone" has nothing to do with gossip – it's because there's a car behind you on an unpaved road.

...when an elevator moves grain and not people.

One Dark and Stormy Night

I'm sitting in my living room in Spearfish, SD listening to the wind howl. And I do mean HOWL… I have never heard such loud, mournful shrieking in my life.

Sure, when I lived in New York City we had "wind tunnels" – huge gusts channeled by skyscrapers down through narrow streets as if masses of air were being pushed by some unseen force through tiny corridors. Try holding onto your hat in one of those…

But this is different: unrelenting, constant moaning and fierce blowing that seem totally unfamiliar. I live up high on a hill, in a "fly-way" clear open directly north. Living here this past year I've become accustomed to the blasts we occasionally get from northerly climes. But nothing ever sounded like this before…

It's evening and my living room shades are down. When I suddenly hear a whack on the side of my house, I decide I'd better take a look and see exactly what's transpiring. I regretfully put down my book and cup of coffee, pull myself out of my cozy chair, and amble over to the windows. The noise gets louder. Much louder. As I start to raise the shades I pause – these winds really are something. I decide instead to pull a small section of shade away from one of the windows to peek outside. Yes, I know this sounds ridiculous – I am, after all, a grown woman – but those winds sound absolutely ferocious.

Whoa – what a scene! Direct from "The Wizard of Oz!" Outside there's a nightmarish mash of debris flying completely sideways from the force of the wind; rolling garbage cans and covers; pieces of airborne trash, twigs, branches, and 2x4's – all mixed together with some kind of grey or beige, occasionally pink, fluffy stuff. Can't even begin to imagine what that is! And long pieces of paper floating all over. All I *do* know: this isn't your regular everyday wind.

My lights suddenly go out. Damn – no electricity. I lift my landline telephone receiver and hear dead silence – no service. My cell is silent as well. And then I hear another airborne missile strike my house yet again.

Could this possibly be a tornado?? There's a restaurant in town with a mural showing the one and only tornado to ever hit this area. Am I witnessing history in the making?? Nah, I think – I'm letting my imagination run away with itself.

But when I hear another thwack, I corral my big rolling desk chair into a long foyer – the only place in the house without large glass picture windows. I find my Ipod (God bless batteries), hunker down in the chair, shut out the moaning winds with the sound of soothing music, and eventually doze off. I wake an hour or so later, pop out my earbuds, finally hear quiet, and trundle off to bed.

Next morning as I walk into the kitchen for wakeup coffee I hear a group of voices outside. I figure gardeners are having a strategy conclave – it's their day for beautifying the town-house development within which I currently live.

Coffee done, I head for the shower. My doorbell rings. Naked, I wisely decide not to answer.

My doorbell rings again. I don't hear the gardeners, and since I'm fairly new to the area and don't know many people, I'm not expecting anyone. Hmmm, maybe someone canvassing door to door? I ignore the bell and proceed to the shower to do my thing.

As soon as I start to towel down, I hear my doorbell ringing insistently – who could possibly be so rude as to sit on my doorbell like that? I throw on a robe and, annoyed, go over to my front door and yell "Go away!"

The doorbell chimes again.

I return to my front door and yell "Go away!" a second time. As I start to leave I hear a deep, commanding, male voice yell back at me, "Lady, open the door!"

I hale from New York City – we do NOT open our doors for a person unless it's a known relative or friend, or an expected delivery. I hesitate, and yell through the still closed, locked door "Who's there?"

And I hear this deep imperious male voice announce "The Sheriff!"

Now I'm really annoyed, thinking this is a neighborhood teen pranking the New York City transplant. I shout back "Go away – you're not funny. And stop ringing my bell! If you don't leave me alone I'm going to call the police!"

Silence…

And then I hear a weary, resigned voice. "Lady, I'm the Sheriff – I *am* law enforcement. Open your door. I have to question you about last night."

I push the shade aside and peek through the glass panel on my front door. Sure enough, there's a huge guy in a funny precariously perched hat and tan uniform standing on my front porch. He has a big etched five-pointed silver star shining on his chest. Just like in the movies. He has a gun hanging on his hip. Just like John Wayne. And this guy not only looks official, he looks damn serious and pissed as hell at me.

I crack the door open an inch. "Are you really a Sheriff? I thought those guys went the way of the 'talkies.' I didn't know you were still out here."

Totally exasperated, he ignores my comment and waves his arm towards my driveway. "What do you know about this?" he demands.

I open the door a bit wider, and am dumbstruck. There, sitting squarely in my driveway is a huge, stripped bare, entire roof eave of a house. And looking down the block, I see a corresponding cavernous yawning hole in the roof of a corner home. What's more, a smaller eave is sitting smack in the middle of the road that used to sit atop the house on the opposite corner. A large group of neighbors are clustered about discussing the situation – ah, the voices I heard earlier.

I politely (now that I know he's a bona fide Sheriff!) ask when he thinks my driveway will be cleared since I have a dental appointment in a couple hours and will need my car. He looks at me incredulously. "Lady, I sure don't know where YOU were last night, but all of us here in town were blasted by a tornado. Every piece of equipment is out trying to clear roads, and telephone and electrical lines. You're in for a long haul – we're gonna need some real heavy duty machinery to lift that eave off your property. I was just checking you were OK." And with that, Mr. Sheriff rides off into the proverbial hills…

So I call the dental office in Rapid City, forty-five miles away, and explain I have to cancel my appointment because part of someone's house is sitting in my driveway and I can't back my car out of my garage. The receptionist laughs and says "Well, I've been working here for thirty-three years. First time I've heard THAT excuse!"

The following day I get a call from the same receptionist. She apologizes profusely. Seems the Spearfish tornado was the lead story in the Rapid City Journal and the accompanying page one photo was of my home, with my neighbor's huge stripped roof eave sitting smack in the middle of my driveway. All the whacks that hit my house were beams that had torn loose from the wayward structure. All the flying grey, beige, and pink fluff, and floating long strips of paper, were insulation whipped from the beams.

It took three days to get my car out. When the crews arrived with a dumpster and a huge derrick to move the eave, I served everyone coffee and cookies.

Including John Wayne…

YOU KNOW YOU MOVED TO SOUTH DAKOTA FROM NEW YORK CITY...

...when a tie refers to kids' sports results rather than something men wear around their necks.

...when a pick-up is a truck, not a guy chatting you up in a bar.

...when talk of "calving" has absolutely nothing to do with glaciers on an Alaskan cruise.

...when a pen is used by cattle, not just people.

Traffic Jam

I loved my new home and adopted state. And I love to explore, especially when fresh experiences are waiting to be discovered. So it was with great glee that I'd hop into my car and go careening about, exploring all the nooks and crannies I could find in the general extended area.

I also love to meditate. I started the discipline years ago to reduce stress when my husband, now deceased, had been ill. At its most simple, the practice allows your mind to take a vacation. At deeper levels, consciousness and abilities can be expanded. When done properly meditation is healing and calming. However, there was one hilarious, unexpected occasion – due to my intrepid exploring – when it proved to be anything but…

Back in New York City, I almost always meditated in the quiet privacy of my Broadway apartment. Way up on the twenty-third floor, the din of the busy streets below almost sounded like a hum.

But it was tough to meditate outside. This is, after all, "the city that never sleeps." And, therefore, it's also a city that's never quiet. Between the rumble of trucks, honking of cars, roar of trains, deliveries, road repairs, emergency vehicles' sirens, overhead airplanes, motorcycles, dignitaries' motorcades, grid-lock, police in vehicles and on horseback, the barking of numerous dogs – not to mention over-enthusiastic revelers – it was really difficult to find a quiet place to zone out when out-of-doors.

Which is one of the reasons I especially loved meditating

in the Black Hills. There were endless opportunities for quiet outdoor contemplation amidst glorious natural settings. And with such a low population (especially compared to New York!), isolation and serenity could virtually be guaranteed.

Well, at least usually…

My backroads ramblings were always a joy. On more than one occasion though, they took me in search of water – the one thing I sometimes missed out here in the middle of the continent. Having always lived within an hour of the Atlantic Ocean, occasionally I'd get a hankering for some kind of wet, blue expanse. Not to swim in, mind you – I don't necessarily enjoy being IN water. I've just always enjoyed being in *proximity* to water. I find it calming, rejuvenating, and inspiring. As such, on one particularly lovely summer's day, this newbie South Dakotan went in search of water out here in the western part of the state. A body of water, specifically, to meditate alongside…

I'd heard there was a dam somewhere north of Belle Fourche, a neighboring town. There was a small sign on a main road indicating its existence, but after that, I was warned I'd be totally on my own. Pre-GPS days, there were no directions or visuals anywhere beyond the one sign. Undaunted, I set off, yes, to explore… Sure, I could have asked a local friend to accompany me to show the way. But that would have negated the purpose of the trip: to be able to meditate alone by water's edge and ruminate on the way home. So I naturally decided to go it alone.

Checking a couple maps, I found the main road past Belle and, en route, eventually saw a fairly sizable body of water a ways off to my left. It was beautiful – a wide expanse of deep blue rimmed by low red clay cliffs, with the sun shining brightly above, reflecting and sparkling upon the water below. Pure heaven…

There even seemed to be a boat dock for fishermen. At a distance, from the road, it appeared fairly busy – not a good prospect for meditation. So I drove past, along the unmarked roads, hunting for a way to approach the water, always turning left to try and get closer. The boat dock couldn't be the *only* water access, could it?

Twists and turns… Backtracking… No street signs of course. A rutted dirt road – more like a path, really. The last house a good fifteen minutes back. Compare that to New York City's meticulously created grid pattern!

And suddenly there it was – the huge wall of the dam, directly in front of me. Could I find my way to the side of it? More meanderings and eventually, success! Careful not to drive into deep holes in a pitted, pock-marked, barely-discernible ascent to a little cliff overlooking the water, I finally sighed with delight at my find – a perfect, isolated, totally silent perch overlooking the waters of Orman Dam.

Bliss…!!

Double bliss, actually… As I turned my head to take in the lovely view, I suddenly saw, pictured in my car's left side-view mirror, a perfect reflection of Bear Butte, Sturgis' sacred Native American site. Not knowing where I was directionally at this point – being so turned around from all the unmarked roads – I simply couldn't believe it! It was as if I was being shown I'd found my perfect meditation place.

I sat in the car for a few minutes soaking in the lovely views and downing a snack I'd brought along. Then it was time for the main event, the cause of my crazy search. I climbed out of my car; walked to a low, ground-level little rock outcropping; sat and wiggled my tush into a comfortable spot; settled my arms and legs accordingly; and after appreciating the beauty of the entire setting again for a few minutes, closed my eyes to start meditating.

I was so relaxed, so happy. My mind just floated away… And as often happens when one goes into a deep meditation, "the world" just seemed to dissipate. Sometimes it's even possible to hear a few strange noises, see surprising images, or smell unexpected aromas.

Which, after a while, is exactly what started to happen…

Way, way, far away – seemingly somewhere off to my right –

I heard the tiniest tinkling sound of a few faint bells.

I'd heard bell tones before in other meditations so ignored them.

The bell tones got a little louder. And then louder still… Deep in meditation, I still ignored them.

After a while there was a faint odor. But I'd also experienced strange smells before, so ignored this as well.

Then the odor got stronger and I realized this wasn't a particularly pleasant smell, whereas all other odors experienced were perfume-like.

The bells continued getting louder, almost as if they were a bit closer. Their profusion was strange…

Just as I was starting to consider bringing myself out of meditation, I suddenly got a distinct whack on my shoulder.

"What the heck??" I blurted.

My eyes flew open.

And there I was, sitting flat on the ground, looking up at a bunch of cows' behinds, getting hit on the shoulder by an errant tail. Simply put, I was seated on the floor smack-dab in the middle of a huge cattle traffic jam!

Do you have any idea whatsoever how absolutely HUGE a cow looks from a ground-level perspective? Especially from the perspective of a city-someone who'd never before even been near a cow? Or how terrifying it was to find myself encircled by at least fifty of these seemingly massive, monolithic creatures? If I got up would they freak and charge? If I started walking back to my car, could I get crushed between a couple of them?

An even greater conundrum: was there a bull in the batch that could wreak havoc?

Oh my, what to do… But at least I understood the reasons for the unpleasant odors and constant tinkling sounds – all the cows wore bells around their necks!

The traffic jam became more dense as dozens of additional cows moved into the immediate area – reminded me of being stuck in Manhattan on New Year's Eve. Or like I was a little sports car, low down to the ground, completely besieged by tractor-trailers, garbage trucks, and huge RVs.

But then I realized I was beginning to hear tinkling sounds off to my left. Which meant the herd was probably moving *through* the area; the traffic jam surrounding me just might dissipate naturally with time.

Aha! Maybe I should just – literally – sit this bizarre situation out and let the cows do their thing and pass on.

And so I had one of my most memorable SD meditations to date. Not exactly the quietest or deepest, or greatly revelatory, but certainly one of utmost surprise. That left a lasting impression…

…it definitely was the largest "group meditation" I was ever part of!

YOU KNOW YOU MOVED
TO
SOUTH DAKOTA
FROM
NEW YORK CITY...

…when a "good suit" refers to Deadwood, not your Sunday best.

…when you discover corn dogs and prairie dogs aren't found in a pet store.

…when a "hot" item just came off a BBQ grill – it didn't fall off the back of a truck.

…when "Type A" is your blood, not your personality.

Potluck Central

OK, I admit it: I'd never gone to a potluck, never made a casserole, and certainly never owned a slow cooker. And now I live in South Dakota, aka "potluck central." Cooking and entertainment styles sure differ from East to West!

What did we do in New York when a bunch of us all got together at someone's apartment? We "ordered in!" With the thousands and thousands of restaurants in NYC, there were loads of reasonably priced "mom-and-pop" places only too happy to deliver whatever your heart desired. Actually, whatever your taste buds desired…

Besides, all the kitchens in New York City apartments are way too tiny for any real serious cooking. (Good excuse, right?) Most are the size of closets with one small counter to house your toaster oven, coffee maker, blender, can opener, and mini grill. So where's the space to chop and mix? Where's the space to even assemble the food you want to cook? Moreover, many of the buildings in the city are quite old – so good luck finding enough outlets for all your electrical doo-dads.

And honestly, if we set up a buffet in the dining area of an apartment (usually part of the apartment's entranceway or living room because real estate is so expensive) then, generally, there'd be no room for more than four guests!

Most New York City kitchens are really crafted only for breakfast – residents grab a fast coffee or yogurt in the morning. We're actually cooking if we make toast. And the rest of the day? Well, we eat out, or "bring in…"

But in South Dakota it's a whole different story.

First of all, when I moved here from the Big Apple, not one restaurant delivered food. (Progress: twenty years later my small home town has a couple places that deliver!). So I was *forced* to start cooking again. Yes, you read that right: if I wanted to eat… *forced*. Having been widowed a number of years earlier, I hadn't actually cooked anything for a while. That's NYC, and that was the only good thing that happened as a result of my husband's untimely passing – I closed my kitchen doors and hung up my apron for good. Or so I thought at the time…

By default, South Dakota changed the scenario – and my mindset.

I was invited to my very first potluck. At a real ranch. Way out in the boonies on a night so dark the rancher left his car's lights on at the entrance to his private road so guests could find his house. In addition to the owners' home there was a bunkhouse for hired hands. Wow! Just like in the movies and books I've read…

I was actually truly anticipating the potluck – figured I'd get to taste some authentic local specialties. The reality: I couldn't recognize half the dishes on the buffet table and couldn't eat the rest due to a personal food sensitivity – salt. Good Lord… A lovely spread, but just not for me. I really, literally, couldn't eat a thing. There was a platter of cheese chunks, some shredded meat mixed with a salty thick white sauce in a big slow cooker, a huge bowl of a cold light green gelatinous something, another bowl of a cold, white creamy something studded with mini marshmallows, breadsticks encrusted with salt, potato chips and real spicy guacamole, corn chips and even spicier salsa, and Crescent Roll salami pinwheels. It was salt-city!

I did a lot of the "pushing things around on my plate" dance that night…

And for dessert? A huuuuge platter of donuts. That's another thing – I'd never eaten a donut until I moved to South Dakota. One more local quirk: nobody ever serves decaf coffee out here.

Yes, I went home hungry that night. But it goes both ways

– I have yet to make a dish to bring to a potluck that locals like. Try as I may, slave as I might over the stove – no one eats what I cook.

Tastes are so very different East to West…

My first potluck attempt was a salmon mousse. A big crowd pleaser back in NY when I used to serve an hors d'oeuvre in my apartment before we, of course, went out to a restaurant for dinner. Expensive. Lots of work. Hard to remove, after it had set, from the tin mold with the hole in the center that I used to fill with grapes. Surrounded with crisp crackers. Served with a knife to delicately slice a piece of the mousse to eat atop a cracker, garnished with a grape or two.

Key word here: delicately.

The first guy that lit into this treated it like a dip, like guacamole, and collapsed the entire carefully-orchestrated circular creation. The startled, accosted grapes all rolled clear across the table, some even venturing further onto the floor. Then he said "Ugh, fish…" And that's how I discovered another thing about South Dakotans – most people here don't like fish.

OK – scratch one…

Second attempt: I decide I'll try a dessert - my real special dark chocolate mousse. (Yes, if you haven't noticed, I like mousses). Real good quality chocolate (melted in a double boiler), lots of cream, lots of eggs – and you beat the hell out of everything with a hand mixer, seemingly for hours. When your arm gets numb you know the mousse is perfect.

Potluck comment? The man sitting opposite me at the July garden get-together, not knowing I was the chocolate mousse's creator, turned to his wife and said "This is real funny tasting chocolate pudding. Think the sun spoiled it?"

I mentioned I had made the chocolate mousse and assured him it was fine to eat.

True story, I kid you not…maybe two/three years later, I notice some woman looking at me askance in the bank. I don't know who she is. But then she walks up to me and announces "I thought I recognized you! You're the lady that made that funny tasting chocolate pudding at Pearl and Don's potluck a few years ago…"

Everybody loves pasta, right? And, seemingly, everyone eats tuna fish. Third potluck attempt: a cold green pepper/tuna/pasta salad. Shoot – guess I'm a slow learner. I really shouldn't have attempted something with fish again, and who knew a lot of people out this way dislike cold pasta…

Three strikes and I'm out.

My quintessential potluck solution? I'm now known as the lady who can always be counted on to bring cheese and crackers to any gathering. And then if no one's happy they can blame my local supermarket.

BUT – oh, how I LOVE my slow cooker. That thing is freakin' magic. Really, don't know how I managed to live so long without one. You can throw ANYTHING into that pot at night and *voilà*!, next morning heaven's awaiting – you waft via the aroma and your nose directly from your bedroom into the kitchen…

The only problem – I tend to eat everything up before I can get the goods to a potluck!

As for casseroles, well, I've decided my life is kinda like a casserole: you take all these disparate elements, mix them all up, and shove 'em in the oven for a while where they're subjected to an onslaught of some serious heat. Miraculously, if nothing gets burned, out comes something harmonious…

One last very important update: donuts are pretty darn good…

YOU KNOW YOU MOVED TO SOUTH DAKOTA FROM NEW YORK CITY...

...when bullshit refers to an actual bull's shit – not some yapping about absolutely nothing.

...when being up at dawn means farmers getting OUT of bed instead of club-hoppers getting INTO bed.

...when X and Y are cattle brands instead of generations of young adults.

...when you're complimented on your outfit and it's your pickup, not your clothes.

Wildlife

I'm creeping up Tinton Road in Spearfish, SD at the city's mandated max speed of twenty-five mph. It's autumn. The air is crisp; leaves are turning gold. The sky's a brilliant blue; the sun is blazing. A perfect day for an outing.

I've decided to head up to the lake outside town for a last visit and ramble before winter's arrival. What could possibly go wrong when the world feels in such perfect alignment?

As I'm tootling along peripheral vision catches movement in some tall grasses to my right. Not to worry. I've been living out here in the West for a while now; am getting used to the myriad wild creatures, small and large, with which I cohabitate. A little different from New York City, my former home, where I'd lived directly on Broadway. The only wildlife seen thereabouts were ubiquitous pigeons perched atop bronzed generals' heads or squirrels terrorizing toddlers in city parks. And, of course, the all-night crazy club kids.

Movement in the grasses again… Maybe pheasant. I do believe hunting season opens soon. Mmmmmm…sliced pheasant breast, served medium rare with lingonberry sauce, an area specialty I absolutely love. Getting hungry – makes my hastily fashioned lunch PB&J sandwich tossed into my purse seem pretty tawdry.

Movement again to my right as I bump along the unpaved road. Turkeys perhaps? Had seen a gaggle or two in the past few days. They'd better take care – Thanksgiving is around the corner.

OK – movement again. What the heck? Show yourself, for

God's sake! I'm not THAT used to living out here yet! Too early in the day for deer. Besides, don't think they'd be crouching along…

Uh oh, crouching along…a mountain lion? Good Lord, is a mountain lion stalking me? Well, not exactly me – my car? Could be a neighborhood cat or dog but I'm a bit too far out of town by now for such an encounter. I bet it's a mountain lion. Wow, wait until I tell my New York buddies – they'll never believe me…

…but first the lion has to show itself – or there's no tale to tell!

Had heard there were a couple lions in residence up this way. A friend midway between the lake and town watched one evening – from the safety of her house – as a lion felled a deer not ten feet from her back deck. Worried about her children and pets, she called local fish and wildlife agents who trapped and tranquilized the lion to move it further from town. Wonder if it's returned…

Then there was the report of a lion who, through an open basement window, broke into the home of a vacationing couple. They'd left their pets in the basement while gone. No sign of them when the couple returned, but a security cam sure caught the lion's gruesome activities.

Whew! Maybe this isn't the best day for an outing after all. I'm thinking if this mountain lion keeps following me I really shouldn't get out of my car…

I keep driving though, against better judgment. Periodically there's still surreptitious movement to the right. Real consternation is starting to set in. And then the movement suddenly veers and turns towards my car. I am definitely not a happy camper at this point!

Slightly frazzled by this time – certainly fueled by my imagination and ruminations – I stop the car. Right there in the isolated dirt road I come to a halt. No way on this rough grade could I safely outdrive something so swift. So I roll up the windows, lock the doors, and wait.

OK, I whisper under my breath. *Let's get this gig on and over with.*

And then I absolutely freak as two huge indistinguishable specters, side by side, rise up out of the tall grasses about ten feet from where I'm sitting. At first my mind – a city gal's mind – can't register what I'm seeing. A wall of blotchy greens and tans starts moving towards my car. Atop the wall are two round circles encased in dark brown from which copious twigs and leaves are cascading. Vines are wrapped about the top of the wall. Faces – once I finally realize these are probably two men – are completely obscured since they've been smeared with a thick grease. Talk about camouflage! And then, as if I wasn't already shaken enough, I completely freeze when I realize that one figure is holding a huge rifle – pointed at me of course – and the second is carrying a really serious-looking "Hunger Games" bow and arrow, ready to let loose at any moment.

I come from New York City, the home of fabled – and sometimes mythical – muggings. Ingrained panic sets in. OMG is this a hold-up? Or worse? It's so isolated out here. What do these scary looking creatures want from me? How long have they been tracking me, waiting to make their move? In a split second, scores of horror movie scenes flit across my addled mind. With one hand I start fumbling in my purse, searching for my cell-phone to call for help. With the other I reach for the ignition key to get going again.

But what if a bullet or arrow pierces my tires and prevents my escape?

I glance up to see if my attackers have moved closer to the car. And then, unbelievably, I watch as two big white toothy smiles spread across the frightening camouflaged faces. One figure pulls off his twig and leaf trimmed brown ski hat; the other raises an arm in a Queen Elizabeth wave. My brain clicks and starts to unfreeze. Images of James Bond commando types and military mercenaries start to dissipate. I suddenly register what I'm seeing: two young men, maybe sixteen/seventeen, greeting me, real friendly as if nothing in the entire world is amiss. A beautiful red-setter proceeds to bound out of the woods and playfully jumps up to greet his owner. I finally realize these are just two young neighborhood guys out hunting for an afternoon.

One starts to speak. As I crank my window open an inch – only an inch just in case – I hear a very polite "Hope we didn't startle you ma'am. We saw an early deer out there on the ridge, past the road, and were tracking it. But then you came along and it started to move away. We tried following him but he took off. Hope you're having a nice day." And with that, the two, twig and vine arrayed, accompanied by dog, head for the woods.

I guess my imagination occasionally shifts into high gear. But speaking about gear, these guys really took their outfits a bit too seriously. Yes, it sure is a wild life I'm living out here with all the wildlife in the wild west. And since at this time of year I'll probably be the sole person up at the lake, I'm thinking maybe I'd better scratch my jaunt, just in case that mountain lion that's been tracking me all day finally decides to pay me a visit...

YOU KNOW YOU MOVED TO SOUTH DAKOTA FROM NEW YORK CITY...

...when a "night out" means just that – camping under the stars rather than "doing the town."

...when "following the sun" signifies a field of sunflowers instead of snowbirding.

...when "pheasant under glass" means a scope, not a five-star restaurant's evening special.

Winter Wonderland

My first autumn in South Dakota. Just lovely – leaves turning, a crisp little chill in the air. A lovely drive into Rapid City, forty-five miles east of my home town of Spearfish.

I'd been shopping at the mall in Rapid, but decide to stop for an early supper before driving home. As I leave the mall and head over to a nearby favorite restaurant, I pass one of Rapid's local movie theaters and see that a film I've been wanting to catch is playing. Showtimes are listed outside the theater above the movie's promotional poster. I happily notice the timing is perfect – I can get a bite to eat and then see the early evening showing of the film before returning to Spearfish.

Dinner is delightful, and I head outside to return to my car. A few passing snowflakes float by. Not to worry – there was no snowfall forecast for this evening. Besides, it's October second – it's not like it's December or January.

The clock has yet to be turned back an hour from Daylight Savings Time, so it's still light, with some waning sun. I pause, enchanted, to watch the ethereal, sparkling snowflakes flecked with gold dancing in the sunlight. I'd seen the phenomenon a couple days before when a few flakes breezed by and was amazed – I finally understood why Christmas cards always showed gold sparkling snow! Coming from the East Coast where snow was always heavy, kind of grey, and laden with water, I'd never seen glistening golden snowflakes before.

But it's movie time, and off I trundle to the theater to enjoy a bit of escapism – with nary a thought to the weather. After all, the movie was just two hours long, I'd seen only a handful of snowflakes and no one had forecasted a storm. Why shouldn't I go see the movie? Why should I head home instead? What could possibly happen in such a short period of time?

OMG - BIG MISTAKE!! It seems while I was sitting, relaxing, and thoroughly enjoying myself in the movie theater, innumerable angry sky gods were ferociously busy at work conjuring a freaking blizzard to wreak havoc on a totally unsuspecting world.

HOW could so much snow fall in just two hours when all I'd previously seen was a half dozen flakes?

HOW could forecasters completely miss a storm of this magnitude?

Most important, HOW was I going to get home???

The snow was already above my ankles as I left the theater. I consoled myself with the fact that I had a new car with new tires – so ostensibly, there was nothing to fear.

I proceeded to prepare to do battle with the sky gods…

As I brushed copious layers of freezing, wet, white stuff off my car's windows with my bare hands – gloves certainly weren't needed when I'd left that morning – a friend's warning about keeping an emergency pack stashed away in my vehicle for winter onslaughts reverberated in my head. I'd planned to get with the program, but geez, it was only the beginning of October!

I slowly and carefully headed onto the Interstate. I was dismayed to see I was the absolute only car on the road. Nothing was plowed yet. Not even sanded. It was hard to see where the road ended and shoulders, or worse, grass began. And what if I got stuck? I didn't even have my emergency pack to see me through.

Snow was whipping every which way. Even sideways. Huge gusts of wind shook the car. My windshield wipers couldn't keep up with the onslaught. Visibility was nil.

I inched along at ten miles an hour. At this rate it would take me four hours to get home! And nobody had ever warned me that as you drive west and north to Spearfish from Rapid

City, as the elevation gets higher the snow generally gets worse. So here I was, ultimately, in a seemingly end-of-the-world scenario.

I finally devised a plan. I stayed in the left hand lane and kept my window open. With my head partially hung outside the window I nearly froze to death, but found – though I couldn't see where the road started or ended – I was able to sense the depression in the center island that separated oncoming and ongoing traffic. And for what seemed like an eternity, that's how I navigated.

Then suddenly, a saviour! Just ahead of me a sander pulled onto the Interstate. I gratefully pulled into his tracks, and dutifully and safely followed this godsend – traveling at about fifteen miles per hour – until I came to my exit. The actual exit sign was illegible; it was totally blanketed with snow. But up on a rise the barest outline of a huge, familiar building let me know I'd finally arrived home.

And yes, it took almost three hours to do so…

Yep, it sure was a winter wonderland out there – you wonder what the hell you're doing outdoors; you wonder why it's snowing like this at the beginning of October; you wonder where the heck so very much snow came from all of a sudden; you wonder where the frickin' road is; you wonder who hired the weatherman and, most importantly, you wonder if you'll ever make it home!! Last but not least, you wonder if you'd lost your senses when you decided to stay in Rapid "just for two more hours" to see a movie…

PS: My emergency car pack now sits in my auto twelve months a year. I'm a quick learner…

YOU KNOW YOU MOVED TO SOUTH DAKOTA FROM NEW YORK CITY...

...when Walmart becomes your shopping mall and Cabella's your favorite boutique.

...when oats, barley, and soybeans are livestock feed – not health food fare.

...when Eastern philosophy refers to Sioux Falls' views rather than yoga and meditation.

...when you don't have a cold, but keep tissues in your car anyway – oh, those long drives with no rest stops.

Melodrama

Most of my writing years ago was commercial in nature.

From contacts made over time, every so often I'd receive a call to travel either abroad or here at home in the U.S. for various tourism-related purposes. Often these requests were last minute.

A good old-fashioned melodrama ensued after one such request when I first moved to South Dakota.

Logistically, when I lived in New York, these trips were almost always feasible. Extensive flights to all corners of the world were always available from multiple airports and a wide variety of airlines. Trains and buses from the city could take me anywhere in the United States. ATMs for last minute cash were outside banks on every other street corner and in airports.

Before the creation of ATMs, I used to keep a cache of trusty Traveler's Checks – globally accepted – stashed away for last minute trips in case I received a sudden call or had to leave over a weekend or holiday.

And then I moved out to South Dakota, arguably one of the more isolated areas in the U.S. Certainly one of the least populated. And most assuredly, underserved by airlines that levy really high fees for tickets. Needless to say, it became a bit more difficult to coordinate those last-minute trips of mine – especially when overseas travel was involved.

Not to mention the vagaries of South Dakota weather and simply being able to get to the airport…

One day not long after I'd permanently moved to Spearfish, a call came for a trip here in the states about a week hence. Not to worry; plenty of time to prepare. I booked a flight online and started planning which clothes to pack.

And then I found myself enmeshed in what seemed like a real true-to-life melodrama! Definition: *a melodrama is a dramatic, sensational, and emotional play.*

The harrowing setting. As often is the case out here in the Northern Plains in winter, the weather abruptly pulled a switcheroo. A massive, previously undetected snowstorm was looming. *True peril.* Fearing I wouldn't get to the airport in Rapid City; that the Interstate might even be shut down; or, if I was lucky enough to get to the airport, my flight wouldn't be able to take off, I decided to move my departure date up to try and miss the storm.

Heightened tension. It was a Saturday afternoon. I'd been scheduled to leave the following Wednesday. The storm was approaching around eleven Tuesday night. *My run for safety...* I needed to leave SD no later than early Tuesday afternoon.

Complications and plot twists. I called my airline. After an endless wait on the phone, I finally spoke to a REAL VOICE rather than a recording, and explained the situation and urgency. But no departures were available on Tuesday. The sole seat available before the storm struck was for Monday morning at six a.m. *Heartfelt emotion.* Oh God, how I hate those early morning flights! I'm never functioning fully at that time of day! Nevertheless, I grabbed that last seat, just grateful I'd "get outta Dodge" in time.

The heroine of the melodrama (me) gets frantic. Yes, there's always a frantic heroine in every melodrama. My brain went into hyper-drive. I'd had days to prepare but was now leaving in thirty-six hours. I threw some dirty clothes I'd need into my washing machine, started pulling stuff from my closet to pack, and yanked my valise out of my back deck storage space.

The melodrama's pivotal scene. Then, with dawning realization, I stood stock still – I had no money!! I'd been warned that some merchants, restaurants, and a few hotels at my somewhat isolated destination didn't accept credit or debit cards, and no one accepted out-of-state checks. *The horror.* I only had about fifteen dollars in my wallet! Pre "street" ATM days out here in Spearfish, I'd been planning to visit my bank on Monday to withdraw some cash for the trip, as well as the local AAA office in town to replenish my Traveler's Check stash.

But now neither place would be open before I had to leave for the airport. *The helpless heroine…* What to do??

I checked online: Rapid City Regional Airport had no ATM. No information was available regarding an ATM machine at my arrival airport. My bank didn't have a branch where I was headed. *The really helpless heroine…*

…searches for a saviour. In a panic, I phoned a couple friends and explained no bank would be open before I had to leave early Monday morning and, at the time, there was no ATM machine in Rapid City's airport. I desperately needed a few dollars. New to the area, this was quite embarrassing. *More emotion.* But one lovely woman (*an angel?*) took pity on me and agreed to meet at a local coffee shop the next day, Sunday, at noon. She had about twenty-five dollars on hand she could lend me. I jumped at the offer – a little something to tide me over until a proper ATM transaction could be effected somewhere.

So there I was, on Sunday at noon, eighteen hours before take-off, about to have coffee with *my angel* in our local coffee shop. When she arrived I jumped up, and with a big hug, thanked her for – *serious drama here* – saving my life!! We proceeded to discuss my melodrama and then she handed over the coveted twenty-five dollars. Even though it wasn't much, at least it was a cushion until I could make some arrangements at my destination. I was so grateful! *Drumroll emotion.*

And then…*the plot thickens…*

While waiting for my friend, totally preoccupied thinking about my imminent departure, I'd neglected to notice a man who'd entered the coffee shop. He inconspicuously proceeded to sit directly behind me. He'd evidently been eavesdropping a bit because suddenly I felt a tap on my shoulder. I turned around and, though he looked somewhat familiar, I couldn't put a name to the face or place the man.

"Excuse me," the face said. "I couldn't help but catch that New York accent and hear about your dilemma."

Perplexed, I asked "Do I know you?"

His answer: "We met a few months ago at my bank when you opened your account. I'm the President. Do you remember that nice conversation we had about my trip to New York City last year?"

Umm…well…yes…

He continued, "I think I can help solve your problem."

Me: "But it's Sunday and the bank is closed. How?"

Him: "It's my bank; I have a key; there's an ATM in the lobby. It's right down the road. Care to join me??" *My SAVIOUR appears! All true melodramas have a saviour…*

Me, incredulous: "You're gonna open the bank on a Sunday for ME?"

Him: "Well, not the entire bank. We don't want to go setting off any unnecessary alarms. But I can certainly open the exterior doors to help you access our lobby ATM."

In total shock, I returned the twenty-five dollars to my equally incredulous friend and, accompanied the President, *my Saviour and the hero of this melodrama*, out the door and down the block to his bank. Where, true to his word, he unlocked the front door and I was able to access an ATM.

Only in South Dakota! (*Note: good melodramas always have a happy ending!*)

YOU KNOW YOU MOVED TO SOUTH DAKOTA FROM NEW YORK CITY...

...when corn rows are in fields and not on the heads of trendy fashionistas.

...when B&B means a "Bed and Breakfast" instead of shopping at Bloomies and Bergdorf's.

...when the latest haircut refers to sheep shearing.

...when "going the extra mile" means you didn't stop for gas at that last service station.

Remembering Laura

I'd bought some land in South Dakota, my adopted home state, with the intention of building my dream house.

This house was pretty specific. Having been an Interior Designer in New York City, I knew exactly what I wanted. So after some preliminary sketches, I hired an architect I knew back east to help the dream become reality.

Since the land in the Black Hills comprised two separate lots of ten acres each, there actually were numerous sites on which the house itself could be built: on a bluff; looking out onto the road; facing inward towards the woods; in a ridge; within a circle of aspens; way up on a hill, and so on. Confused as to which site would be the best choice, I couldn't make a decision regarding an actual building location.

The architect came to my rescue. Having never before seen Mount Rushmore, he decided to use a bunch of frequent flier miles for a free ticket to sightsee western South Dakota with a stop at my nearby land to help me choose my building site. His one perplexing directive for me prior to his arrival: "Go to a hardware store or garden shop. Buy four of those armed eight/ten dollar plastic outdoor chairs. You're gonna put them to good use."

And so Frank arrived. He brought with him some tall wooden dowels with orange flags attached and, pulling on sturdy boots, we proceeded to trek through each lot – planting a dowel wherever a possible building site existed. My instructions: while Frank visited Mt. Rushmore and some other nearby attractions, I was to revisit the lots as often as necessary to limit my choices to two sites per each piece of property. He'd approve my choices upon his return.

Easier said than done. I'd chosen these lots because they were so beautiful – it was really difficult to eliminate locations. But after a couple days while Frank was touring, I was finally able to winnow the possibilities to the four he requested.

Then came the hardest part – the final decision. When Frank returned and approved the four choices as structurally sound, I was instructed to place one of the four plastic chairs I'd purchased in each spot, smack dab in the middle of the woods. And he suggested I sit in each chair twice over the next few weeks, for a minimum of an hour each time, to see where I felt most at home.

I practice meditation – have been doing so for many years. "Even better," Frank said. "Meditate in each location. You'll definitely sense which site is best for your personal comfort." And then he took photos and directionals for each of the four locations to help advise my local builders – and left for New York.

I dutifully followed his directions. An initial round of brief meditative stints quickly established preference for one lot over the other. And then I set out one afternoon to try and choose the definitive building site between the two remaining locations.

It was a beautiful sunny spring day, later in the afternoon. I hiked through the lot to the first white plastic chair sitting there, glaringly out of place in the glorious natural, heavily treed setting. I settled myself into the chair, closed my eyes, and started focusing on my breathing. Normally within five/ten minutes I'd be in a lovely, peaceful, altered state of mind.

But, evidently, not today. Something was definitely eating at the edges of my consciousness, not allowing me to "let go." What was it? I could sense a disturbance, but didn't have a clue what the issue was.

I tried again to slip into that blissful meditative silence, but no luck. Was this most assuredly NOT the place to build my new house, or was it something else that was bothering me?

And then I heard it – a long, deep, wailing, soulful "a-ooooo" coming from somewhere to my right.

"OK, some kind of animal," I thought. "I am, after all, in the woods. Got to get used to this."

The wail was repeated a few times and I began to realize an undisturbed meditation was going to be difficult, if not impossible.

But that was the least of my problems: there was suddenly a rapid response to the wail – from my left. And I realized the initial wail hadn't just been a casual sound, but had actually been a "call" to another of the species – and I was sitting smack between the two!

And maybe there were more than two…

And just maybe they weren't that friendly…

I panicked. Safety – my car – was a good ten minute uphill hike away.

Was my imagination running away with me out here in the woods? This was, after all, one of the first few times I'd been out here alone. Maybe the noises were from a group of teenage boys horsing around, trying to throw a fright into someone like boys often did back on the city streets of New York.

But then I realized that wasn't feasible. The entire area was uninhabited – I'd been one of the first to purchase land here and no houses were under construction yet. Moreover, no one could have known where I was – my car wasn't visible from the county's rough dirt road. I was probably a good mile into dense woods.

The only wild animals I was used to back in New York were Central Park's squirrels. I sat in the chair, paralyzed, as I realized two or more animals might be signaling an unwanted human had invaded their territory!

Memories of Laura Ingalls Wilder – an early South Dakota pioneer – came flooding back into my mind. As a child I had devoured all her very popular autobiographical books about living out west. They had seemed so exotic at the time. Very possibly they were a factor in my decision to check SD when I considered moving. But as the responding "a-ooooo" calls on my left and right began to sound closer, I suddenly remembered all the frightening encounters Laura and her family had with wolves in so many of the books.

Uh oh…

Yellowstone National Park, in Wyoming, was only five hours west and grey wolves had recently been reintroduced to the area. My land was less than ten minutes from Wyoming's border. Had the wolves migrated east to South Dakota? This city gal got spooked – I bolted out of that plastic chair with such adrenalin, and charged uphill to my car so swiftly, it was like I was running some Olympic marathon.

Laura and her family had always been rescued from their perilous predators, but out here I was totally on my own. Was I, literally, a sitting duck? Was I making a big mistake?

Friends in town, when I related the story the following day over coffee, laughed at me. "Probably only a couple of coyotes. Wouldn't have come anywhere near you…"

And "Listen, hon, you better get used to company out there in the woods…"

Maybe so, but for a city-bred woman who's only used to hearing the honks of taxis and the rumble of subway cars, those mournful cries sure sent shivers up my spine.

So I figured out how to solve the problem. When my house is complete I'll buy my very own *personal* animal – a really, really, really big dog for protection.

And I'll name her Laura…

YOU KNOW YOU MOVED TO SOUTH DAKOTA FROM NEW YORK CITY...

...when the "melting pot" is a taffy and peanut brittle pan rather than a symbol of different co-existing nationalities.

...when people mountain climb instead of social climb.

...when "burying the hatchet" signifies wood-chopping instead of forgiving an incident.

...when "Rushmore" means the mountain instead of a crazy, hectic lifestyle.

Tinkerbell

I'm charging up the road to the tiny town of Belle Fourche, South Dakota. My left foot's tapping away to the sound of country music on the radio and I'm humming along, looking forward to a night of dancing. Dancing? On a Tuesday night? In Belle Fourche??

Yup – square dancing! When I moved to Spearfish, SD from New York City I intended to experience the real West – in all its glory. So square dancing it is! I don't quite have the nerve yet to wear the ruffled skirts and petticoats, or the studded blouses, or the neck scarves – but I'm sure wearing my dancing shoes…

The music's infectious, the caller's fun, and the people are great. Everyone's out for a good time. In the whirl of ensuing square and circular activity, pros – with the absolute patience of saints – help beginners, who suddenly can't fathom their "right" from their "left" or remember who their partners are. Square dancing isn't just a rigorous physical activity, it requires mental agility as well: it not only demands learning new dance steps but an entirely new vocabulary. For the uninitiated, the caller might as well be speaking a foreign language. For this New York transplant "allemande" and "do si do" were the closest I'd heard, since my move, to the garble of multi-languages prevalent on the East Coast.

Another great thing about square dancing – you don't need to come with a partner. This was particularly good news for this Ms., a recently-widowed Mrs. Everyone dances with everyone in a huge, friendly hodge-podge.

Periodically I'd be asked to partner with a really big, strong, older gent. Tall, broad, and still muscular, he'd steer me around the floor as if he was manipulating a vehicle through heavy traffic; he'd twirl me around as if I was some tiny Tinkerbell. I'm no size six – yet when the caller would yell "Swing yer partner!" this guy would just flip me up and away, off into the wild blue yonder...

Christmas break was approaching. There would be no classes for a number of weeks. As we all said our goodbyes and wished each other a happy holiday, this gentleman pressed a piece of paper into my hand and said, "Check me out on my website."

Excuse me. Hello? What have we here??

Curiosity got the better of me: I tried to log onto his site. As it happens I'd just bought a new computer and had been having trouble with the updated programs. So I called my hi-tech son back in New York City for help. Son gives me directions – no luck – still can't get into the website.

NYC Type A son loses patience with mother's technical ineptitude, but kindly offers to check out the website for her until she can get some local, hands-on computer help. Mom gives son the web address...

Two hours later – from his slick thirty-third floor glass and steel skyscraper office overlooking Madison Avenue – son, in his conservatively tailored grey and white pin-stripe suit, powder blue shirt and navy silk tie, just leaving for a corporate business meeting, takes a moment to call South Dakota.

"Mom," I hear over the phone in a very strange, incredulous voice, as if I'm somewhere out on the moon, as far from sophisticated New York City as one could possibly get. "Mom," he asks in total disbelief, "you're dating an 'ex' rodeo champ – fringe, sequins, chaps and all???"

Takes me a moment to realize what he's referring to...and then, with dawning awareness, I start laughing. No wonder my big, strong square dancing partner could twirl me around like some little slip of a thing – he used to flip cattle!!

I tell my incredulous NY son not to worry – I am, literally, in good hands.

And I guess the rodeo star was looking to trade a cowbell for a Tinkerbell…

YOU KNOW YOU MOVED TO SOUTH DAKOTA FROM NEW YORK CITY...

…when someone refers to "New Jersey" and they don't mean the state – they bought a new cow.

…when chips aren't blue and signify Dow/DuPont stock – they're used in your fireplace.

…when a nail fix deals with a fencepost, not a manicure.

…when spirits refer to sacred beings rather than the drink you just downed.

Celebration Time

My daughter's birthday! A BIG birthday! Certainly cause for a family celebration.

But my son was working in California at the time, my daughter was employed in Washington D.C., and here I was in South Dakota. We were all over the dang country! Where could we meet up for a quick weekend celebration that wouldn't entail long days of flying that would interfere with my children's work schedules? Or have them pay exorbitant plane fares…

We pored over maps and hit on Chicago. Centrally located with reasonably priced flights for my children. As for me, NO air fare from South Dakota is reasonably priced to anywhere. And so, I decided to try Amtrak out here in the Heartland. My first train trek in the Midwest.

When I lived back east I had used Amtrak to various locations numerous times. To Washington DC, Boston, and Montreal for example. Had even traveled all the way down from New York City to Miami with my parents when I was a teenager. And as an adult I'd traveled all over parts of Europe by train.

So it's not like rail trips were new for me. A fairly experienced traveler, I enjoyed relaxing on a train, perfectly content to let someone else take me where I was going. I googled Amtrak; found the closest station in Williston, North Dakota; checked the schedule.

"ONE train a day traveling in each direction? Are you kidding me?" Between Grand Central and Penn Stations back in New York I was used to well over a thousand trains each day!

After recovering from my shock, I bought my roundtrip ticket on Amtrak's Empire Builder and was "good to go…" I was looking forward to the journey, relaxing in a wide-windowed seat from which I'd enjoy rolling views of the Great Plains. What could be better? Armed with a good book for night travel, and some snacks to augment the dining car's selections, I couldn't wait for my little jaunt. And of course, my daughter's birthday bash.

But first I had to get to Williston, ND to catch the train – an easy five hour drive direct north of Spearfish, my home town in SD.

No biggie… The day before I packed the car with my weekender valise and a bag containing a bunch of gifts. I threw in a map just in case. Some water. A piece of fruit. A light jacket. Since it was summer, weather vagaries wouldn't be a problem. Everything was set.

The following morning I left my house by eleven. The train was scheduled to arrive in Williston at 6:59pm, but I wanted to allow sufficient time to make sure I made that train. Wouldn't do to miss my daughter's big celebration… After gassing up I hit the road north, heading first for a town about an hour's distance for a quick lunch. Had heard two women owned a tiny general store there wherein they concocted the most unbelievable homemade soups.

Yes, the soup was delicious, and then I was off again. The scenery was lovely. The day was fine. Everything was going according to schedule…

A bit further north, since I had ample time, I made a little detour to take a look at Medora, perhaps to visit its old town on my return trip and catch one of the site's famed performances. And then I briefly stopped at the southern section of Teddy Roosevelt National Park for beautiful views of the Badlands thereabouts. Having heard the north unit of the park had even more spectacular scenery I decided to add that to my return drive's wish list.

So my meandering into North Dakota continued. Pleasant,

unhurried, with nary a care in the world. Even with all the little side forays, I'd get to Williston to catch the train with plenty of time to spare.

And then, a bit further north, there was a little bronze marker by the side of the road, about 15" high by 20" wide. The type of marker that usually signifies some place of historical significance. I whizzed past, too fast at the designated speed limit to read it. But about a quarter of a mile ahead I suddenly slowed down, pulled over, and stopped the car. Something about that marker was bothering me. I knew I had to back up and read it. Don't ask me how I knew – I just knew.

The road was totally isolated so backing up wasn't that big of a deal. But oh, when I read the marker, THAT was a big deal! I was so shocked I had to read it two, three times for its import to gel in my mind.

The marker casually informed me that I was leaving Mountain Time Zone and entering Central Time Zone.

"Wait, WHAT?!!?

"WHERE??"

In South Dakota that switch took place smack dab in the middle of the state. Didn't that demarcation continue straight on due north? Here I was on the extreme western edge of North Dakota. HOW could the change in Time Zones occur here, a good two hours west of where it shifted in South Dakota?? I was completely stunned, not to mention confused…

…and then dismayed! Because I suddenly realized I would miss the train to Chicago. The one and only eastbound train that came through Williston each day. And therefore I would miss my daughter's birthday celebration.

Here I thought I'd be arriving at the station – in Mountain Time Zone – with almost an hour to spare, and I suddenly discover the train is arriving one hour earlier than I expected according to Central Zone time.

I'm truly a law-abiding citizen. I don't speed. In almost forty years of constant driving I'd received two speeding tickets. En route to my son's college graduation – where he was a featured speaker – due to endless traffic in a huge construction zone, there were interminable delays. So of course, when the road opened up, I started flying a bit to try and arrive at the ceremony on time. Naturally, a cop was waiting and I received my first-ever speeding ticket. As for the second, well, I never even saw the speed limit sign.

So I persuaded myself, *How dare that time zone be so erratic and ridiculous!* The road was open. There'd been no other vehicles around anywhere for hours. I had really good reflexes. Let's go for it…

…and I hit the gas pedal…

No casual meanderings now. White-knuckled, clenching the steering wheel, intently peering ahead, constantly checking my mileage indicator and my watch, I made a frantic run for it.

I pulled into the parking lot, situated directly in front of the tracks, just as the train was arriving at the station. I wildly started honking my horn and flashing my car's lights. As I maneuvered into a parking spot, I caught the conductor up in the locomotive waving at me – he'd recognized the "dash of the desperate" – and I knew he'd hold the train until I could pull my luggage from my car and board.

As I charged to the train, struggling to roll my valise over a ground-covering of pebbles, the ticket collector nonchalantly climbed down to the platform. Panting, sweating, and beet red, I finally reached him and fumbled in my purse for my ticket.

He took one look at me, registered my panic and distress, and calmly asked "First time on Amtrak from this station? Drive north?"

I couldn't even speak. I dumbly nodded my head "Yes."

He laughed. "Had a problem with the time change, did 'ya?"

I looked at him, surprised, and he wryly added, "Congratulations – ya did good. Consider yourself one of the lucky few. This is the only station on the run where we consistently lose passengers…"

YOU KNOW YOU MOVED TO SOUTH DAKOTA FROM NEW YORK CITY...

…when fiddling refers to music, not fixing your company's financial records.

…when a stud signifies a horse rather than diamond earrings.

…when "blue blood" doesn't reference the Carnegies or Astors – means you've been standing outside too long and it's minus ten.

…when "one for the road" is roadkill, not a nightcap!

Elevator Epiphany

Friendliness, neighborliness – both have long been hallowed hallmarks of the Plains.

So it was a bit startling for this New York City gal who'd always been used to complete and total anonymity to discover – when she moved to Spearfish, SD, population 10,000 – that 10,000 new friends awaited.

Everyone belonged to a favorite church, supported a cherished charity, or was a volunteer somewhere. Everyone was part of a school project, or a sports program. No one ever discussed politics or sensitive worldwide topics (or God forbid, argued about them) like opinionated New Yorkers do. But everyone wanted you on their team to aid their beloved endeavors. And so, initially, there were copious amounts of lunches, coffees, and events to meet certain people and learn about different causes to hopefully get on board.

I was invited everywhere. Life suddenly became really hectic…

And then there were the simple little day-to-day friendly gestures. Like a driver's hand, clutching his car's steering wheel. When he passed you he'd briefly raise his pointer finger to acknowledge your existence as you drove by. Note: since you're only driving 25mph in town you can't miss the hello. Or perhaps you'd merit a nod of the head.

Or the post office employee remembering not only your name, but your PO Box number – absolutely impossible in New York City. Or the local dry cleaners phoning you when your clothes are finished ahead of schedule because they think you might need them. Or popping into someone's office without an appointment just to say hi simply because you were in the neighborhood.

It's a whole different ballgame out here...

Not that New Yorkers can't be friendly. Yes, they have the reputation of being aloof. But that's not really the issue. New Yorkers are always crushed, and in a huge rush. There are just so many hours to each day and so much to do in the city during that brief time. So they're always tightly scheduled and constantly on the go. Stopping to chat, to "visit," is simply unheard of.

Early on, when I'd moved to South Dakota, I learned my normal New York "modus operandi" when running errands simply wouldn't work in this area. Say it would normally take me about an hour to accomplish three/four quick stops back east. Here I was lucky if I managed two! Because literally everyone you ran into – friend or acquaintance – stopped to "visit!" Yes, it was lovely seeing everyone and catching up, but I consciously had to readjust my sense of timing and how I constructed each day. Everything here in the West actually takes twice as long to accomplish because everyone constantly chats – no one ever enjoys spontaneous visits back east. Everyone is just too darn busy. What's more, there are so very many people in the city it was really an earth-shattering event if you ever ran into someone you knew!

For the first six years I lived in Spearfish, I kept my New York apartment and periodically shuttled back and forth between the two locales. It wasn't just to make sure I wanted SD to be my permanent home: I still had family back east. And then one day I suddenly realized I'd actually become a South Dakotan! Big shock: I was no longer a true New Yorker.

It was time to sell NY and make SD my full-time abode.

The surprising, determining event:

My apartment was on the twenty-third floor of a twenty-nine storied building. (Actually it was a twenty-eight storied building because there was no thirteenth floor. Lots of skyscrapers in the city ostensibly "omit" a thirteenth floor on their elevator screens because no one wants to live or work on unlucky #13.) I actually only knew one other person in my building other than front desk staff. Tenants might meet when they regularly left for work early in the morning or returned late in the evenings. But, since I was self-employed, my schedule varied all the time – I never consistently bumped into the same people.

Strangers never spoke to each other while in the elevator. Strangers never even looked at each other while in the elevator.

On this particular fateful day I locked my apartment door, sauntered down the hallway to the elevator, and pushed the down "call" button. Waited a bit, and then the elevator arrived. The doors parted to reveal three people within – determined to be a couple and a single from a cursory glance. They'd evidently entered the elevator cab on one of the floors above mine. All three silent, minding their own business, glancing at the cab's floor.

As I stepped into the elevator, I looked at everyone cheerily, opened my mouth into the dead silence thereabouts and brightly said "Good morning everyone. Lovely day, isn't it?"

The three of them looked at me in horror. And I could just read their minds: "Uh oh, we've got a loony locked in here with us."

Slowly, almost imperceptibly, the three edged away from me as I took my place among them.

My greeting at that moment suddenly made me realize it was time to leave New York for good. It was time to say good-bye to impersonal NYC and permanently embrace my 10,000 Spearfish neighbors…

But that simple, unexpected greeting that so naturally popped out of my mouth also made me wonder, "Is friendliness catching? How long before I start wagging my finger at pals when driving?"

YOU KNOW YOU MOVED TO SOUTH DAKOTA FROM NEW YORK CITY...

...when a "good catch" means spending a day on a lake rather than finding the perfect mate.

...when hooting at night is an owl – not some parked car's burglar alarm being tripped.

...when jerky is a salty beef snack rather than the way your silly kid is acting.

...when aromatherapy tends more to fertilizer than New Age remedies.

Double Jeopardy

As a teenager back in New York I was consistently visited by a "Peeping Tom." After I'd return from weekend evening dates, I'd start undressing in my bedroom in my family's ground-level ranch style house, with window blinds drawn and down. But, periodically, I'd hear fingernails grating on my window screen. Not the most pleasant experience...

I'd yell for my father who, enraged, would grab a baseball bat. And in his pajamas, screaming like a banshee, he'd take off after the perpetrator. Who by now, of course, hearing the ruckus, had taken flight. But he always left proof of his visit: a neighbor's lawn chair placed beneath my window.

This went on for a number of months until the Peeping Tom was eventually apprehended by the police.

A negative experience, to be sure. But it actually served me well regarding future incidents in the Big Apple and other locales to which I traveled alone for work – unavoidable in any large city these days. I seemed to have developed a "sixth sense" that alerted me when my personal space was being invaded.

In bucolic South Dakota I was absolutely shocked one night when this sixth sense was suddenly activated.

I was at home in my living room, working on my computer. It sits on my desk, which faces a wall. Behind me, to my left, there was a large picture window. Though I had been gazing at my computer screen, I somehow, suddenly, intuitively, knew something had occurred at that window.

Horrified, I realized it felt as if I was being watched.

Oh God, another Peeping Tom??

I glanced up from the bright computer screen and was surprised to find how quickly time had flown. My work must really have been engrossing. It was bright and sunny when I'd sat down and now the entire living-room and I were both engulfed in total darkness. The computer screen emanated the only light in the room.

Alone in the house, I'd been too preoccupied to draw the window's curtains when dusk fell. And I just *knew* someone was watching me through that bare window – I was certain. All the familiar warning signs had kicked in: there was a very particular heightened awareness, and the hairs on the back of my neck and arms had pricked.

What to do? Pivot on the desk chair and face the person who was watching me from the window? Then what? There was no one in the house to call for help. I wondered how long the person had been watching me and how long he planned to stay. If it was a burglar and he was armed would he shoot through the glass? Should I continue to work, head down, and make believe I didn't know someone was there?

But I'd already completed my computer tasks for the evening.

Maybe the culprit was patiently waiting for me to go to sleep so he could break in and burgle. Worst thought of all: was the Peeping Tom *not* on the other side of the window but *already* in the house, actually standing a few feet behind me??

There was a sharp letter opener on the desk. Aha! Protection! With a sudden burst of resolve and massive charge of adrenalin I grabbed the opener with both hands and swiveled in my chair to face the window and whatever uninvited interloper was invading my space.

The living room was pitch black. Through the window I could see it was an extremely dark night as well – no moon. A perfect night for a prowler.

But when I lowered my eyes towards the bottom of the window, I was totally startled by FOUR huge, round, glowing luminous orbs of light staring fixedly at me.

FOUR? Round? Well, I'd certainly felt something was watching me, but my goodness, what was it?

As my eyes slowly adjusted from the brightness of the computer screen to the dark of my surroundings, through the window, silhouetted by my neighbor's porch light cross the street, I suddenly could distinguish the faint outlines of four pointy ears atop the four shining orbs. And then I realized two deer, noses pressed to the window, were staring goggle-eyed, totally transfixed, at my brightly lit computer screen.

Just like when they stare goggle-eyed at a car's headlights.

Two deer, just hangin' out, as if they were watching TV, looking through my living room window mesmerized by the bright changing colors and shapes on my computer screen.

As repugnant as my New York Peeping Tom experience had been, excuse me, I can't resist – this South Dakota escapade was truly *"endeering..."*

YOU KNOW YOU MOVED
TO
SOUTH DAKOTA
FROM
NEW YORK CITY...

...when a decoy is used for duck hunting instead of a drug bust.

...when squash is something you plant in your garden, not something you play at your health club.

...when "booting up" has nothing at all to do with computers and everything to do with your feet.

...when an auction means cattle and horses, not Picasso and Renoir.

"Enhanced" Dirt

Two hysterically wailing little kids and one bereft mother watched through a rear window of their house as a massive early summer storm with gale-force winds made mush of their first, beloved vegetable garden. It lay their emerging corn stalks flat. Shredded their baby lettuce. Tore beans from their struts.

After all that work! And all the talk about the veggies we'd watch growing all summer long and eat fresh from our garden!

For days my children waited, in vain, for the corn stalks to dry out and pop upright again…

And that was my one and only feeble attempt at a vegetable garden back east in New York when we were living on Long Island.

But then, years later after I moved to South Dakota, I heard a new community garden was being created. Two knowledgeable friends invited this utter novice to join them. I was delighted. Perhaps, with the proper coaching, I could finally learn to grow my own veggies…

But first the earth in the new community garden's little individual plots had to be prepared so it was viable soil. A call went out to all involved with the project to report for work. Both my "plot-mates" happened to be out of town that weekend, so it was up to me – I had no idea what to expect.

I should have immediately realized I was way out of my depth when someone good-naturedly scoffed at me "Hey, New York – you don't have to wear earrings when gardening!" So of course, I proceeded to lose one that afternoon amidst all that dirt.

And dirt there was…piles of it, full of rocks, pebbles and other assorted debris. We were given little wood-framed screens to sift the dirt through. The goal: to wind up with enough good soil to lay over the rough dirt in our plots to assure better growth.

That's when I noticed most people were wearing gloves. But hey, I never minded getting my hands a bit dirty for a good cause… So handful by handful I scooped up the dirt, pushed it through the screening, and discarded any remains.

So much dirt to winnow! There'd easily be two, three more meetings just to get through the piles.

As it neared time to leave the project organizer looked at me and said "Next time you come you really should wear gloves."

When I asked why he answered "Because all this dirt comes from the city dump. It's compost – enriched by all our 'remains.' You really should wear gloves when working with it since we're not quite sure what it's comprised of."

My face blanched. I looked down at my hands. They were caked all over with the "enhanced" dirt. My fingernails are long – the dirt was embedded deep beneath them. I suddenly felt nauseous – *what* had I been scrounging around in for three hours? What microbes had I picked up that might now play havoc with my system? Water wasn't yet installed at the new garden: there was no place to wash. How to drive home and get into my house to soap and water and *disinfectant* without touching anything??

There was a stray piece of paper on the ground, fluttering in the breeze. I picked it up: a bill for some gardening tools. I walked to my car and gingerly used it as a shield when opening the door. I'd left my car/house keys sitting on my seat. A napkin was on the passenger seat, remains of a recent snack. I used it to pick up my keys and start my car, then rolled it around the steering wheel. I drove the short distance to my house with that one hand wondering what horrific diseases my body was absorbing at that very moment…

Using the same napkin as a buffer I hit my garage door

opener and, once inside, closed everything down. Using the napkin one last time to exit the car, I stood there in my garage and totally stripped. Yes, stripped completely naked right there in my garage. No way those microbes were getting into *my* house! I used the clean back of my shirt to open the door to my house – and made a beeline for the shower.

That was one loooong shower. You can bet I exited well-scrubbed.

But my hands still didn't feel clean! Two, three times over the next couple hours I found myself at a sink scrubbing away. I started to feel like Shakespeare's Lady Macbeth.

And then a worse horror presented itself. Come dinnertime, I was dismayed to find I'd left chopmeat and spices in a bowl in the fridge, ready to make into a meatloaf. Oh God, HOW could I sink my hands into that raw meat after what they'd touched all afternoon?? And then eat the result? *Absolutely no way…*

A banana and a container of yogurt worked just fine that night, thank you.

As a matter of fact, it took me three days to finally feel comfortable enough to sink my hands into that meat to shape it into a loaf.

You better believe I bought gloves – two pairs so one would always be on hand (no pun intended…) when the other was being washed.

As for subsequent worms and other assorted garden insects, well, that's another story. Suffice it to say I've become a regular customer at our local summer farm stands…

YOU KNOW YOU MOVED TO SOUTH DAKOTA FROM NEW YORK CITY...

…when carpooling means a dog in the back of a pickup.

…when a trailer is something you live in as well as a preview of a movie.

…when dancing is geometric: square dances, round dances, line dances.

…when "stacked" refers to a pile of pancakes, not a woman's physique.

Broadway Bound

It happened when I was thirteen – my first serious love affair!

That's when my parents, during a weekend get-away, introduced me to the theater. I was totally transported at a little vacation town's "summer stock" performance of "Guys and Dolls." It was thrilling. Always an avid reader, it seemed like a book could suddenly, magically, come alive on stage. Which, of course, is exactly what theater is all about! I was in heaven…

…and I've been in love ever since.

Directly after high school, while attending a nearby college, I started working summers in New York City. So I was able to obtain "student discount tickets" to Broadway shows. When I married, my husband and I would often see performances, and I introduced my two children to the magic of Broadway when they were young. Most New York residents never pay full price for tickets: they belong to different organizations offering discounts or get last-minute day-of-show reduced entry. So the cost, at the time, wasn't prohibitive.

My daughter also grew to love the theater. She moved to NYC after college; I worked in Manhattan. We often caught a play together. If one of us was near the 47th Street "Discount Ticket Booth" in the theater district we'd check its availability board, phone, and buy last-minute seats for the two of us. It was always a spur-of-the-moment surprise and lots of fun.

So, when I announced I was moving to South Dakota, friends and family kept saying "You're gonna miss Broadway! How can you leave New York when you love the theater so much?" My answer: "There are traveling troupes, community groups, and college performances – I'll survive." And so I did. I became an avid attendee of all the myriad productions out here...

As such, late one Friday evening at a charity event in Spearfish, before the close of the affair, there was a drawing for door prizes. I never win anything, so didn't pay much attention. But when the grand prize was announced my ears perked up – two orchestra tickets for Saturday's matinée performance of famous playwright Neil Simon's "The Odd Couple." Part of Rapid City's "Broadway Series" at the Civic Center, I'd been thinking of going Sunday, but hadn't yet purchased a ticket.

And the winner was – you guessed it – me! I was thrilled. Off to "Broadway" again! But I had won two tickets and was only one person. What to do with the second ticket??

A few months back my daughter had moved to Billings, MT. On occasion, hankering for a look/see mother/daughter confab, we'd phone and arrange to meet mid-way in Sheridan, WY for a late lunch and couple hours of gab. Then we'd each turn around and head back to our respective home towns. It was always such a special, crazy, last-minute treat.

Memories of our similar, fun, spur-of-the-moment New York "Broadway days" popped into my head. I decided to take a chance... Would she??

When I arrived home at 11pm, winning tickets in hand, I phoned my daughter. I knew she wouldn't be awake – she's an early to bed/early to rise person. I, on the other hand, am a late to bed/late riser. So I left the message: "Join me for Broadway! I just won two tickets for 'The Odd Couple,' which I don't think you've seen, for tomorrow's matinée. If you leave your house at eight a.m. you'll arrive at my place at twelve-thirty. Lunch will be out on the table, ready to chow down. Then we'll hop into my car at one, to arrive at the Civic Center by two. And *voilà*! – we'll share mother/daughter Broadway again – but this time out here in the West!

"PS – you know I sleep late. Just leave a message whether or not you're coming. If not, I'll call a local friend to join me when I get out of bed."

And I traipsed off to sleep wondering who my mystery partner would be next day…

Sure enough, next morning when I climbed out of bed, the light on my phone message recorder was blinking. I pushed the incoming button and heard "Broadway bound! Here I come! Time for mother/daughter Broadway again. On my way…"

No doubt the truly "oddest couple" at the performance that afternoon of "The Odd Couple" was the crazy mother/daughter duo from South Dakota and Montana who used to live in New York City – one directly on world-famous Broadway itself!

But the funniest part of this crazy escapade deals with the actual trip to the show…

New York City is infamous for its grid-locked traffic. And it's always at its worst just before performances when thousands of ticket holders descend upon the theater district at exactly the same time. It usually took at least an hour and a half to drive thirty miles from the suburbs in bumper-to-bumper traffic. And once drivers hit the city, they'd inch along and get snarled at traffic lights on every single corner. Giving a totally alternate meaning to the term Broadway *bound* – my God, did they get tied up! And after arriving they'd first have to find a parking garage that charged almost as much as their theater ticket!

Out here in the West, my daughter hopped into her car in Billings, zipped three hundred twenty miles to my place at seventy-five miles per hour, with absolutely no traffic, and ONE (yes, one!) stoplight between us. When we left Spearfish for Rapid City one blinking red light separated us from the Civic Center.

So yes, NYC's Broadway shows are unequaled. But Broadway out here in South Dakota certainly comes with its own special perks…

YOU KNOW YOU MOVED TO SOUTH DAKOTA FROM NEW YORK CITY...

...when a "smoking gun" means target practice, not the key witness in a law case.

...when New England clam chowder, Manhattan clam chowder, and Long Island duck are the closest you're gonna get to an ocean.

...when a bug problem is a dirty windshield, not wiretapping.

...when something is rigged and it isn't a shady deal – it's an oil drill.

Lessons

In a very clear dream I was unmistakably told, "You are to carry an eagle's claw to the farthest fir tree atop Bear Butte."

I awakened immediately.

"Oh no," I erupted. "You have GOT to be kidding."

Yes, I'd been thinking of visiting the sacred Native American site once again to give thanks for my fortuitous move to South Dakota. After all, a previous meditation at Bear Butte had been instrumental in my decision to make SD home. But my thanks, *absolutely and most certainly*, were planned for a ground level location. Not only had I never climbed anything more formidable than a big hill, I was well into mid-life and not exactly what you'd call "in shape." I'd also recently had a serious car accident that left me with a broken bone in my left foot.

Moreover, where in the world would someone who wasn't Native American obtain an eagle's claw? I knew it was both sacred and illegal.

Confused by the dream, it nevertheless continued to play in my mind…

***

The Elderhostel program was offered on the campus of a university in a neighboring state. I decided to attend to learn more about the history of the Sioux, the Native Americans indigenous to this area. The five full days of classes covered the background and culture of local tribes, as well as their legal system and struggles with the U.S. government. Various Native

American and Caucasian guest lecturers presented material; a professor who had lived on a local reservation for most of his adult life hosted the program.

Deeming it was "now or never," since at the time I didn't have any Native American friends to ask, I timidly approached this professor at breakfast the morning of our second day, when he was sitting alone over coffee, and asked if he knew where, or from whom, I could obtain an eagle's claw. And lest he think me totally crazy, I hurriedly explained my need. To my absolute surprise he very thoughtfully answered, "I will consult with the Hawks at dawn and get back to you."

Well, he didn't "get back to me" for the rest of day two, nor for that matter on days three or four. And I hesitated to approach him again, feeling I had imposed. But then, just as I was saying goodnight the last evening of the program, the professor approached and said, "I have arranged for a 'sweat' tomorrow on the reservation after the end of our classes. You will be given what you need after the cleansing."

I was in shock; I was thrilled.

After the "sweat" – a very moving and enlightening experience – I was ceremoniously handed something wrapped in bright red fabric. As I opened the package, tears came to my eyes – it was a large bird's claw embellished with beautiful thick brown, cream, and white feathers attached by strips of deerskin. And the professor said, "We cannot give you an eagle's claw, but this is an owl's claw and wing. The owl is known as the 'night eagle.' When I consulted with the Hawks they said this would suffice."

***

Having procured the necessary night "eagle" claw I decided, one fall afternoon the following year, to try and climb Bear Butte, actually the remains of an ancient, extinct volcano. My foot had mostly healed, the weather was coolish, and the sun's strength was mitigated by wisps of clouds. "A perfect day for an outing," I naively thought. I wasn't quite sure what to take with me – other than the night "eagle" claw as mandated. I slipped it, wing and all, still wrapped in its ceremonial red fabric, into a slim canvas bag I could sling over a shoulder. At the last minute I threw in a small bottle of water and a flashlight. Though weak – heaven knows when the flashlight had last been used – the light did shine when flipped on.

I arrived at the Butte and set off, up the mountain. Quite jauntily at first. The path was fairly wide and level; the pebbles, stones and exposed tree roots pretty minimal. This initial part of the climb is readily accessed by non-Native locals and tourists, as well as Native Americans who leave prayers – their entreaties signified by colorful fabric strips tied to tree branches. As the wind blows through the trees and the strips of fabric rustle, it's felt the prayers are repeated over and over for Creator to hear.

After a while, the path started to narrow, get steeper, was much stonier with more difficult footing, and I saw that the prayer strips were beginning to thin out. But I was on a mission and labored on – what, for goodness sakes, had my dream been all about?

A smarter, more savvy outdoorsperson would also have noticed that a lot of climbers were already beginning to come *down* the mountain, and no one was ascending either in front or in back of me.

But I was so preoccupied with the arduous climb it was as if I was wearing blinders!

After what seemed like endless trudging, at times with rolling stones and no foothold, and me occasionally scrambling on all fours, I was absolutely delighted and relieved to see the summit of the mountain up ahead. And then, as I approached, my heart sank – it was *not* the end of the trail, the path just did an abrupt jog to the left and kept going on and on.

I made a snap decision to continue – I knew if I stopped at this point I would never return. This was proving far more difficult than expected.

More climbing, totally alone, really difficult now, but I finally reached the summit, where a small redwood deck had been built. As directed, I hauled my aching body over to the far corner of the deck overlooking all the trees. And then this totally obtuse city gal – with her dream in mind – gazing at a mass of trunks, branches, and leaves, helplessly asked "OK now, which one of these is actually a fir?"

But there was no response. I could hear no other voices; see no other climbers. I suddenly realized how completely isolated I was. Instead of delivering the suitable, respectful prayer and thanks I'd planned in these auspicious and very beautiful surroundings, in utter bewilderment I shrieked, "What the hell am I doing up here???"

***

In addition to giving thanks, I had originally planned to meditate atop Bear Butte if it wasn't too crowded. But with all my attention focused on the actual physicality of reaching the summit, I never did realize how much time had passed nor did I realize that dusk was already beginning to fall. There was no time to waste, it was imperative I start my descent. Down was always easier than up, I reasoned, so I was certain I'd be back in the parking lot in no time at all.

Wrong.

Down proved a challenge of another sort. I kept skidding on myriad little pebbles that tumbled as I stepped on them. Already tired, I found I had to keep my wobbly knees bent to try and gain leverage. Dusk swiftly turned to dark and I had difficulty seeing the trail. There was a sliver of a new moon and I was so grateful for its light – until the trail twisted and the moon was hidden by the hulk of the mountain. Then everything was pitch black and silent – except for the roll of pebbles underfoot.

I gingerly rummaged around in the canvas tote for the old flashlight, praying for a beam. Otherwise, I would have to spend the night out here on the trail, high up on the mountain where it would be cold without a jacket. Miraculously, the flashlight activated and a weak, slim beam of light tremulously outlined the path two feet ahead. Very cautiously I started to descend again. I prayed the flashlight's batteries would hold until I reached bottom.

A couple minutes later the flashlight dimmed further. I was horrified. It was so dark. I tried descending with tiny baby-steps – at this pace it would take me hours to get down – but found even this wasn't feasible. I stopped dead in my tracks, figuring I'd have to stay the night. I just hoped there were no mountain lions in the immediate environs.

So much for trusting and following my dreams...

So much for attempting an outdoor activity on the spur of the moment, without sufficient preparation...

And then, all of a sudden, drumming started. Loud. Pulsating. Multiple drums. It was strange – I couldn't tell what direction the sound was coming from. Unexpectedly, I felt compelled to try to descend again to the sound of their beat. As I very slowly twisted round the mountain following its downward path – with my dying flashlight in hand – the drums didn't wax or wane: their sound stayed level regardless of where I moved. Even stranger, as I eventually climbed lower and was finally able to discern a faint outline of the parking lot down below, I saw only one parked car – mine.

I reasoned that some Native Americans were in a different section of the mountain – open only to tribal members – celebrating something or praying. All I knew was that I was grateful for the drums: I didn't feel so alone.

Then the flashlight abruptly died. I stopped again, afraid to move. But the drumming continued, pushing me forward. Soon the path began to widen a bit, and wasn't quite so stony. For the first time I actually began to believe I would make it home that night.

I still heard the drumming – loud and insistent. And though absolutely no one was anywhere near me to see, the very exact instant my left foot touched the level ground of the parking lot the drumming ceased.

Complete silence.

And yes, my car was still the only visible vehicle.

During the ensuing week, I ran into a new Native friend who often prayed at Bear Butte. I asked if any tribes had been to the mountain the previous weekend and she said no, it was the wrong time of year for vision quests. I explained what happened. She smiled and replied, "The mountain is truly sacred, you know. The Grandfathers' spirits drummed you down. Maybe that's what your dream was trying to teach you..."

I understand – especially after that night. But I always seem to get into scrapes out here – like a real fish outta water.

So to the revered spirits, here's an updated prayer:

"Sincerest thanks, from the bottom of my heart, for all your help. I'm truly most grateful. But please, could you possibly keep an eye on me in the future? Seems I need a little guidance now and then – at least until I earn my own wings ..."

YOU KNOW YOU MOVED TO SOUTH DAKOTA FROM NEW YORK CITY...

...when a snow job refers to removal, not someone trying to pull the wool over your eyes.

...when "fritter" connotes corn and apples rather than wasting time.

...when a woman's "glass ceiling" is a kitchen greenhouse, not a corporate stumbling block.

Zapped

When people say you "slow down" living out West in contrast to the East Coast's hectic pace, boy, they're not kidding. At one point my daughter and I just about became catatonic!

She was living in Billings, Montana at the time. Though she loved the area, her career eventually necessitated a return to New York, home base for our family. However, while she was residing in South Dakota's neighboring state, we often met midway at area attractions for a day, or planned periodic weekends away together.

Hence, our little weekend trip to Thermopolis, Wyoming to savor its luxurious, salubrious, thermal waters. Time to de-stress, relax, and spearhead a little healing! Thermopolis – Greek for "hot city" – is billed as "the world's largest mineral hot springs."

Day one, Friday: we each left our respective states, drove to the little town somewhat in the middle of Wyoming and, mid-afternoon, checked into our motel. We were sharing a bedroom with two beds.

After our arrival we did a little tour of the area, especially interested in seeing the town's beautiful mineral deposit formations. We made sure to stop at the local public pool and bath house to make appointments for the following day and check on protocol for participation. It's believed the hot springs are part of an underground thermal system emanating from Yellowstone National Park. Outposts of these healing waters even exist in Montana and South Dakota.

We'd both truly been looking forward to this trip. On one

of our many previous overseas jaunts, we'd visited the Dead Sea in Israel. But though we saw numerous people relaxing in its healing waters, since we were on a day bus excursion to the area, time precluded a dip. Ever since, we'd always wondered what enriched waters felt like or how they could enhance one's well-being. The people "taking the waters" in Israel couldn't stop lauding the benefits of the Sea – it was filled with so many minerals they couldn't even submerge. They all just floated by, their bodies naturally absorbing whatever essences they needed.

I'd also visited a number of Eastern European countries where mineral baths are actually considered legitimate, medical regimens called "Balneotherapy," recommended by certified doctors. Karlovy Vary, in particular, in Czechoslovakia (now the Czech Republic), is a beautiful spa town with quite a few such sophisticated clinics – as well as public bathing opportunities. Free spigots for drinking the city's healing waters are available in numerous locations around town. People actually walk from site to site, holding cups and glasses to refill as they imbibe.

Meanwhile, in Thermopolis, my daughter and I had brunch on Saturday and, after a suitable wait, we headed over to the hot springs facility with much anticipation. We learned the waters fluctuate from the mid-90s to over one hundred degrees and contain at least twenty-seven different minerals. My daughter chose to submerge in the steamy public pool. I preferred something more private: a dip in a tub in my own small cubicle. We were asked if this was our first visit and then, because it was, we were warned not to stay submerged for more than twenty minutes.

We both looked at each other, skeptical, thinking the same: "A little extreme, don'tcha think? Hyping the experience a smidgen??"

Anyway, we each cleansed under a shower, grabbed a couple towels, and then my daughter left for her pool while I headed for my tub.

Mmmmmmm…total deliciousness…the body just floating…the mind dead to the world…silence…EXCEPT for the clock tick-ticking away, set to buzz at exactly twenty minutes to remind me to exit the tub.

DING! and I climb out, really sorry to leave my little cocoon. I head to the showers to once again wash down. My daughter is nowhere in sight. Worried, I'm wondering if she's still in the pool. As soon as I dress I hurry over to check, and sure enough, there she is, in the water. I motion to her to leave, pointing at my watch. She very reluctantly does so; she also loved the experience. I tell her we'll meet at my car.

While she goes to shower and dress, I return to the front desk to make appointments for the following morning, Sunday, before we're each scheduled to drive home to our respective states. And then I walk outside, headed for the parking lot.

Well, I sure didn't get too far. Right in front of the building, maybe fifteen feet from the front door, is a bench. Certainly strategically placed, it was all I could do to make it to that bench to plunk my so-slowed, so-relaxed body down, because it was mush and couldn't stand up on its own accord! My brain also seemed like mush...

This was a level of relaxation beyond relaxation. What was in that water??

I kinda just sat there, in a funk of a stupor, for a couple minutes. And then I heard my daughter's laughing voice as she exited the bathhouse, "Mom, what's with you? Hot springs get to you?? Or are you just gettin' old on me?"

I dumbly nodded my head yes to all accounts and watched as she jauntily came down the steps towards me. And then, after a few feet, her face suddenly changed as her entire body became jelly-like. She looked at me with wordless shock, struggled forward, and slowly, silently, slid onto the bench next to me.

And there we sat, the two of us, totally catatonic, without saying anything, for at least fifteen minutes.

I finally managed to say "Don't think I can do what we'd planned for this afternoon. Think I need a wee bit of a nap."

Me – the person who never, ever naps during the day.

She nodded her head in agreement.

And then, "Just hope I can drive us back to the motel…"

The two of us sat there on that bench a little longer. Eventually, laughing at our slowed-down/slow-motion/life in the slow lane selves, we managed to haul our super-ultra-relaxed bodies over to the car and then up to our room. Very uncharacteristically, we each dropped everything we were carrying on the floor as soon as we entered, and climbed onto our respective beds still fully clothed, anticipating a half hour nap. We were dead out in seconds…

Yup, we reeeeally slowed down…

FIVE HOURS LATER I felt a hand nudging my shoulder and heard a groggy voice, "Mom, wake up. We haven't eaten since eleven. It's a small town. All the restaurants are gonna close pretty soon. We have no food in the room. We have to get something to eat."

Forcing my eyes open, I couldn't believe how dark our room was. Where had daylight gone? And then I glanced at the night-table clock and did a double-take. Still in a bit of a fog I mumbled "Twenny minutes. I was only in that tub for twenny minutes…"

After a couple tries we found a place still open to catch a bite to eat. Thank God for their very strong coffee, loaded with caffeine. It snapped us out of our zap. We actually felt terrific once we rejoined humanity. But much as we loved the mineral water experience, and discussed returning at some point, we both knew we had to cancel our appointments for the following morning. There was just no way we'd be able to drive a number of hours home directly after another visit.

So to set the record straight: it's not simply an advertising slogan when it's said western living offers a slower pace and is more relaxing. A visit to the area's hot springs confirms it!

Life in the slow lane – you betcha!

YOU KNOW YOU MOVED TO SOUTH DAKOTA FROM NEW YORK CITY...

...when a stampede refers to buffalo rather than store openings on Black Friday.

...when the sound of honking indicates geese rather than grid-locked cars.

...when "line dancing" doesn't mean you're number six hundred waiting to use the Ladies' Room during a Broadway show's intermission.

Buddy

People here in the West are unbelievably friendly. Unlike New York, there's no hesitation in approaching a stranger any place, any time.

Therefore, in the middle of a fresh veggie aisle in my local supermarket – as I paused in front of the brussels sprouts – I wasn't really surprised when an older gent suddenly turned towards me and asked, "How do you cook 'em?"

My answer: "I steam them, then add a little butter. Or sometime I cut them in half, mix in a bit of olive oil and black pepper, and roast them."

He smiled and said, "I bake mine with a good Sunday roast, with potatoes. Really tasty eatin'!"

"I bet!" I said, as I chose a few of the little green guys and proceeded to move on down the aisle.

To my surprise, the guy followed behind me. When I paused in front of the string beans he commented, "Not too fresh. I wouldn't buy those if I were you."

There are plenty of farmers out here in South Dakota, as well as folks who just love growing their own food, so I figured the guy – in his blue jeans and plaid shirt – probably knew what he was talking about. I thanked him for his expertise, didn't take any beans, and moved on.

Suddenly I discovered I had a "buddy." My commentator moved from behind me to directly alongside me. At which point I noticed he wasn't pushing a basket full of food items.

I couldn't quite fathom what he was up to. I looked around for his "better half," but he seemed to be alone.

And so began a very bizarre shopping experience in the fresh fruits and vegetable section of my local grocery store. My "companion," almost like a toddler sticking close to Mom and her shopping cart, never left my side. There was a running commentary on all the produce for sale as I wended my way through the cauliflower and beets, on to the oranges and nectarines, then over to the tomatoes and onions, finally winding up at the potatoes.

He was in his element here! Boy, did he know his potatoes. Not only those on display, but dozens of other varieties and colors as well – and prices for all…

So he was appalled when I only chose two largish spuds for baking.

"Look at this red mesh bag here completely filled with taters," he said. "These are half the price of what you're buying."

"I'm only one person," I protested. "I don't use potatoes that often." And then I realized he'd mentioned cooking his Sunday roast. Was this man divorced or a widower, looking for company? Since I was a widow had he noticed my ringless finger?

A freaky thought flitted through my mind: *Was he shopping with me like he'd previously shopped with his wife?*

I suddenly got uncomfortable, especially when he tried to pressure me into buying the bag of potatoes in his hand. My next thought: *Were the bagged potatoes local and was he the farmer who'd grown them?*

Regardless, I declined…

Fifteen/twenty minutes had already passed, yet he continued to walk alongside me, chatting away, as I segued over to the eggs. At which point I turned to him, thanked him for his help and suggestions, but said I really had to rush now to finish my shopping list. Then I abruptly turned my cart and moved off into another section of the supermarket.

He didn't follow me, and I was grateful. I didn't want to hurt his feelings, but I also wasn't interested in his company.

Came time to check out. The man was nowhere to be seen

as I approached a register and unloaded the items I'd stashed in my cart. As usual, after paying my bill the cashier proceeded to place my collected goods in plastic bags to transport to my car. When finished, she reached for a large red mesh bag of potatoes I hadn't even noticed at the far end of her counter. She put them into my cart, next to my bundles.

"Wait a minute," I said as I stopped her. "Those aren't mine. They weren't in my shopping cart and I haven't paid for them."

"I know," she answered. "But a man was here a little while ago and *he* paid for them. He gave me instructions to send them home with you."

"Excuse me?"

Recovering from my shock, I wondered how my buddy could possibly have known which register I'd be using to check out.

But the strange encounter didn't end there...

I told the cashier I appreciated the kind man's gift, but rarely used potatoes. I asked if she'd please keep the bag and, when an elderly person or a shopper with children came along, to please give the potatoes to them. She agreed, and we left the red mesh sack of potatoes at the end of her register, awaiting new owners.

I returned home, unloaded my car, and started unpacking my groceries. Imagine my surprise when I opened one of my numerous bundles and found, sitting inside, the big red mesh sack of potatoes my buddy had paid for. I *knew* the cashier and I had left that red mesh sack on her counter for others...

I'll never understand how I wound up with all those potatoes, and I never saw the man again to thank him for his gift.

But I sure hope *he* found a "buddy" to share his Sunday roast – someone who loves potatoes as much as he does!

YOU KNOW YOU MOVED TO SOUTH DAKOTA FROM NEW YORK CITY...

…when the "daily special" is a local café's meatloaf, not a racetrack trifecta.

…when perks and benefits refer to fresh coffee and "2 for 1" muffins rather than corporate incentives.

…when logging has to do with tree cutting as well as signing in to your computer.

Just Sayin'...

When tourism first opened to the People's Republic of China years ago, my late husband and I jumped at the opportunity to visit. Aside from interest in the people, culture, history, scenery and sites, my husband, a dentist, specifically wanted to see how authentic Chinese acupuncture was performed. He'd heard the practice could be used for such serious dental procedures as root canals without anesthetics.

He filled out a lengthy "special request" form – necessary to allow us to deviate from a set, approved tour – that was submitted to the Chinese government. Lo and behold, we were OK'd for a hospital visit, with translator/guide, to observe an acupuncturist at work.

What an experience! We entered a room about thirty feet square where rows of bare pallets accessible by ladders were stacked three high on all four walls. Every single pallet was occupied. People – all still sporting the ubiquitous blue Mao jacket – were in various forms of undress with needles protruding from every conceivable place in their bodies.

In the center of the room, at a battered old desk, the acupuncturist was attending a little girl of about seven who had severely crossed eyes. The child, with needles protruding all around her eye sockets, stood quietly and nonchalantly, singing to a doll in hand, as the acupuncturist continued to insert needles into her face. Through our interpreter we learned how many millimeters her eye muscles had already shifted, and how many more treatments and months were necessary until her eyesight would be normal. The only recourse, in Western medicine, would have been delicate eye surgery.

We watched the acupuncturist work on a half dozen more patients, and we were sold!

Back in New York, after copious research, I located a practitioner who'd been trained under a Master Acupuncturist in China, and for the next few years no matter what my problem – including a need for surgery – acupuncture always took care of my issues.

But when I moved to Spearfish twenty years ago, I discovered acupuncture was unheard of in South Dakota. I was bereft – it was such an incredible health boon. And then I learned there was a practitioner in Gillette, Wyoming, an hour and a half distant. Someone who'd actually studied in the Orient…

So began my frequent treks back and forth to Gillette over the years. After a while, I actually began to look forward to the drive. The scenery was lovely – an open road peppered with long stretches of isolated country, loads of gentle rolling hills speckled with buttes and cattle, and a seemingly endless big blue sky – something you'd never see back in New York City. Accustomed to all the skyscrapers crowding Manhattan's skyline, I never tired of watching South Dakota and Wyoming's scenery fly by my car's windows, or the areas' brilliant blue, sunny skies with their lazy and wispy or big fluffy clouds.

One particular beautiful spring day – country music blasting on the radio, windows partially open to enjoy the fresh breezes – as I so often did on these drives, I happened to glance up into the sky. A perfectly clear blue sky. But this sky had a very peculiar white cloud in it. It didn't seem to be floating. It just sat there, implacable, a solid white chunk of a cloud suspended in the blue, seemingly unmoving. No other clouds were anywhere else in sight. And this cloud had a peculiar shape, like a squat bell.

When I first moved to the area I'd heard some weird stories about South Dakota and its environs – about strange lights atop Devil's Tower (which I happened to be near at the moment), and aberrant magnetic areas reported by telephone line installers. And yes, there were one or two comments regarding strange sightings in lonely, isolated areas. But I'm a pretty level-headed person and don't ascribe to any such stuff.

Yet, this strange, very tactile-looking cloud seemed to just be sitting there, suspended in the sky. There wasn't another cloud for miles in any direction. And it didn't float about in the wind or shift and change shape as clouds usually do.

I was so surprised – this cloud, of all things, started to make me feel uncomfortable. And I found, as I was driving – alone – I kept glancing up periodically to check it out. Yes, it was still there, in the very same location. At one point I actually got a bit paranoid – when I glanced up it suddenly felt like the cloud was looking back at *me*! I started getting uneasy – I'd been the only car on the road, in both directions, for a while now. At the same time I started laughing at myself!

And then, suddenly, the cloud just disappeared. I'd glanced down to adjust my radio dial due to some static. Took no more than a split second, but when I looked back up into the sky that strange-looking, implacable cloud was gone. Big, totally empty, deep blue sky – nothing more…

I was so shocked my hands started shaking. Here I was, a grown adult, gettin' spooked. It was as if someone had thrown a switch from on to off: one second something was up there and then immediately it wasn't. "Clouds" just don't "go out." They float by, they wisp, they transform into various shapes – they don't just disappear in an instant.

I have no idea what really happened that day. And I self-consciously laugh about my strange reactions every time I recall the incident. But in actuality there are so very many things we tend to shut from our minds, or refuse to consider plausible, unwilling to stretch our frames of reference…

…like slim painless needles inserted in specific bodily points to alleviate pain and effect healing. Or the possibility there just might exist other forms of sentient life more advanced than we are.

Just sayin'…

YOU KNOW YOU MOVED TO SOUTH DAKOTA FROM NEW YORK CITY...

...when a pool party means some cue sticks at a local roadhouse rather than a dip at the Country Club.

...when fire retardants refer to forest fires, not your kid's PJ label.

...when white collar isn't a job description – it's a shirt heading to a wedding, funeral, or church.

...when "57" connotes a squirt of ketchup instead of a world famous street full of galleries and boutiques.

Thor

One of the things I absolutely love about western South Dakota is its lack of bugs. Yes, if you're hiking or camping out in the woods, you're gonna run into a lot of these pesky but necessary tiny critters. But on the whole, day-to-day, the average person lives relatively bug-free out here.

Coming from the East Coast, that's a big change. With all the water in the area, mosquitoes were prevalent spring through fall. Termites were always an issue. Silverfish would climb up out of ancient plumbing into sinks and tubs, and roaches lived in the walls of most old New York City buildings – especially those located above restaurants and supermarkets. And then there were the carpenter ants who looked harmless enough but could go through your house struts in no time at all. Not to mention the spiders – unwelcome any time of the year except for Halloween.

On the other hand, where I live out here in the West, amazingly, there are just three bug-related issues each year. More amazingly, each for a very short duration. Somehow flies know, before anyone else anywhere – and especially our weather forecasters – when winter is about to set in. Though you haven't seen a fly for months (unless you happen to work around horses and cattle) – and you certainly haven't had one in your house all year long thus far – suddenly flying missiles invade your personal territory, zinging here and there in your warm and cozy home, anticipating some chill in the air to which only they are attuned. Miraculously they eventually become sluggish so are easy to eliminate. But how they find entrance when doors and windows are shut is an eternal mystery.

And then there are the mysterious two days each spring when, after perfectly normal circumstances, you awake to find the air absolutely teeming with cringe-worthy flying creamy-winged creatures. The very first time I experienced this, it felt like a Biblical onslaught. They attach to everything; make it impossible to drive; and squish like hell on your windshield. Man, is it tough removing the sticky oily remains! Ugh...

Last but not least, we have the mysterious Box Elder beetles. Like the flies, you never see the little black creatures, but suddenly one day there they are – creeping up a window pane, on the tile floor near an exterior door, on a window sill. At least they don't move that fast so they're easy to catch. But they have a hardish shell so make a nasty ick scrunch when they meet their maker.

As you can tell, I'm not a fan of insects. But lest I sound completely heartless, I want to state that I have a pact with them. Outside in the open air they rule; they take precedence; I would never harm the tiniest creature I encounter. However, my house's interior is a different matter entirely. This is MY territory and, if I want to sleep at night, bug be gone or I'll make sure of it!

The one serious thing we don't have back east that I did encounter out here in South Dakota was a rattlesnake. Visiting the Badlands on my own, I pulled into an empty parking lot at a scenic stop on the sightseeing loop. It was a warm, sunny summer afternoon. I opened my SUV's door, pivoted to exit, had my left leg out of the car ready to step down – and literally froze, breath suspended. Directly under my foot, coiled, sat a rattlesnake baking on the hot asphalt. I hadn't noticed anything as I pulled into the parking spot, but there it was – this colorfully-marked coiled circle with a shaking upright tail. Thank God I was in a tall SUV and not a low little car! I VERY slowly lifted my leg higher and shifted back into my seat. I couldn't close the door fast enough! Though a little shaky from the encounter (after all, I was traveling alone, no one was around, what if the rattlesnake had struck??), I did back the car out of the spot and pause to check the creature out. It was really hard to believe such an interesting looking little thing could be so dangerous. But there must be some ingrained snake karma most of us carry around because after a big shiver, I left that parking area – where I'd planned to do a little hike – and decided to head to another spot. I wasn't taking any chances of meeting up with the rattlesnake out on the trail somewhere.

One summer's day this past year, in my own house, I was sitting at my kitchen counter eating dinner. Totally relaxed, gazing across my living room at the lovely mountain views visible through the large glass picture windows straight ahead, I happened to glance down at the bookshelves directly beneath. And then at the light beige carpet in front of the bookshelves.

Something had caught my eye. Something was there that didn't belong. A long thinnish blackish/brownish strip. About eighteen inches or so. A piece of ribbon? Too thick to be a piece of cord. I couldn't imagine what it was, where it had come from, how it had gotten there. I casually climbed down from my kitchen stool, ambled over to take a better look, and at about three feet distant stopped dead still. At close range, I discovered it was thicker at one end than the other and it had diamond markings all along its length.

SHIT – it was a snake. A BIG snake. In MY house!!! The absolute nerve…

Good Lord, what to do?? I live alone so there was no one in the house to help. If I tried to phone my next door neighbor for aid I'd lose sight of the intruder – not a particularly good idea if I ever wanted to feel comfortable in my house again!

"Oh God," I suddenly realized, "I'm gonna have to kill this thing myself…"

But with what? My two standard weapons to vanquish invading flies and beetles seemed ill-suited for the job: my trusty fly swatter was too flimsy; even a rolled magazine didn't seem strong enough to do sufficient damage.

Keeping my eyes on the snake I started to step backwards – and suddenly it took off like the proverbial bat outta hell. OMG this darn thing moved so freaking fast! I was startled; I was horrified; I was miserable... This thing HAD to go!!

In my kitchen there was a drawer, behind where I'd lazily and happily been enjoying dinner a few short minutes ago. In this drawer were some tools – specifically, I recalled, a hammer. A good, strong hammer. More importantly, I could back up to that drawer without taking my eyes off the pernicious snake so he couldn't just go and disappear into some nether region of my house.

Hammer in hand – like the mythological god Thor descending from heaven to wreak justice on evil – I advanced towards the snake. I swear this thing was telepathic – it totally knew what I was planning. Completely still until I approached, it suddenly took off again and started zig-zagging here and there all over the place with the speed of Japan's famed bullet train. I wondered, "Who's more afraid of whom?"

And then a crazy, exhausting dance ensued for a good twenty minutes. There are two black leather sofas facing each other in my living room, with a patterned wool Navajo area rug between them atop my carpeting. This damn snake's reflexes were so very much faster than mine. First he took refuge under one sofa, and when I moved it to try and find him, he slithered under the area rug. When I flipped the area rug up, he sped under the second sofa. Then back and forth, and back and forth some more. And all the while I'm running after him, constantly lunging at his slip-sliding disappearing shadow, while brandishing my hammer in desperation, swinging it through thin air onto my empty carpet!

I sure was a candidate for the TV show "America's Funniest Videos." But this, in my mind, was no laughing matter: what if the snake was poisonous?

At long last, I hit the tippy end of the repugnant creature's tail. It instantly shriveled up. I was totally appalled, but hoped it would slow the devil down. Once again it took refuge under one of the sofas, I guess to nurture its wound. As I slowly pushed the sofa aside even more, I simultaneously executed a huge lunge forward and finally brought the hammer – Thor's avenging tool – smack down on its diamond shaped head.

I could actually see its beady little eyes and pointy teeth.

…and then blood exploded all over the place – on the hammer, on my lovely beige carpet, on the light grey paint on the wall! I was so absolutely, so completely, so totally grossed out…

Like its tail, the rest of the snake slowly shriveled up, atop my blood stained carpet.

Breathing heavily, I sank into a living room chair. What an ordeal! This had resembled an epic battle between two arch enemies. And now it was time to bury the dead. But I somehow couldn't bring myself to return to the combat scene, hidden from view behind one of the askew sofas.

And then I remembered a friend was coming to visit the following day. A friend who had grown up on a South Dakota farm. SHE was no doubt familiar with snakes and wouldn't shrink from dealing with the last of this nightmare.

So I returned to my by now ice-cold dinner. Of course couldn't eat a darn thing. And never looked nor walked behind that sofa for the next twenty-four hours.

When Sue walked into my living room the following evening she was shocked at the disarray all over – until I wordlessly led her to the battleground site. And when she saw my nemesis and bloodied weapon of choice – Thor's hammer – she broke into peals of laughter, and sympathetically and efficiently took charge to bring my trying encounter to a close.

Periodically, on facebook, parents post proud pictures of their growing kids out hunting, celebrating their "first kill." My first kill will always be remembered as a day of infamy, will never be celebrated, will never be remembered, and will forever remain anonymous…

YOU KNOW YOU MOVED TO SOUTH DAKOTA FROM NEW YORK CITY...

...when getting hitched doesn't mean a wedding – someone's tying up a horse somewhere.

...when a hot spring refers to thermal waters, not ninety-five degrees in May.

...when a "winning streak" suggests Deadwood instead of a buff sprint across the Mets' baseball field.

...when "having a cow" implies the herd's increased rather than someone having a conniption.

Seafood Withdrawal

So I absolutely love seafood. And oh, did I miss it!

New York, where I was born and bred, is one of the greatest "foodie" destinations in the world. Due to the city's docks on the Hudson River – which leads directly into the Atlantic Ocean – and a healthy shipping industry, innumerable tons of our oceans' riches are disgorged daily from boats, barges, and trawlers destined for the bellies of hungry local diners.

These docks are a hop, skip and a jump from the city's famous Fulton Fish Market – destination for the best of the seas' delicacies. Here's where you'll find the most famous chefs – from New York's lauded four and five star restaurants – trolling in the wee hours of the morning when fish and seafood are first delivered. All of them searching out the most fresh, most rare specimens. Endless rows of all kinds of oceanic delicacies, displayed on ice, greet buyers and sightseers. Just be sure to hold your nose when wandering – it's not exactly a perfumery you're visiting.

Chinatown is nearby, another mecca for fresh fish and seafood, with open stalls spilling onto streets from noisy "mom-and-pop" shops.

Further uptown where I used to live are two huge, famous, specialty food stores – one of which carried, daily, an unbelievable selection of fresh fish and seafood from all over the world. Like forty-seven different varieties of oysters… Or distinctive types of clams from bays I'd never even heard of… Fish whose names I couldn't pronounce… Purple lobsters...

My apartment was across the street from this hallowed

emporium. What a delight to roll out of bed and pick up a "just caught" piece of fish or seafood for dinner – fresh off the docks!

And then I moved to South Dakota – home of beef, more beef, and even more beef. Not to denigrate red meat, but needless to say, at one point I seriously got depressed from what can only be described as seafood withdrawal.

It was difficult, when I moved here twenty years ago, to even find a restaurant with fish on its menu. And when I'd innocently ask, "Is the fish fresh?" I'd always get a yes. Only to find that "fresh" in this neck of the woods meant fresh-*frozen*. And frozen fish in no way tastes like just-caught fish.

And so it was with absolute delight, when traveling with my daughter who was visiting out here in the West, that I noticed a poster advertising a "Rocky Mountain Oyster Cook-off Competition." I totally LOVE oysters! So does my daughter. The two of us immediately decided to detour a bit from our sightseeing plans to indulge our passion and have lunch at the oyster cook-off. In actuality, we were really hoping there'd be some raw oysters on ice, our favorite way to imbibe.

In the car we had a "remember when" moment. A few years before, on a sightseeing jaunt down in South Carolina, the two of us were walking along a row of adorable little restaurants fronting the coast. We passed a sign advertising "Fresh Oysters: $8/dozen." We promptly pivoted and charged into the place – oysters in NYC cost upwards of $2 apiece! We each ordered a dozen, finished them off, and resumed our walk. Half a block away we simultaneously stopped, looked at each other, laughed, turned around, walked right back into the restaurant – and ordered another dozen to split! Such is the stuff of fond memories – and good eatin'!

With this in mind, salivating, we headed to the Rocky Mountain Oyster Cook-off Competition. We wondered where these oysters originated since we were nowhere near a coast. Were they cultured in huge vats somewhere? Were they flown in specially for this event? Would people be around to help shuck them from their shells?

We pulled into the advertised town and followed the crowds to the cook-off's location – a large parking lot filled with loads of booths. Competitors, busily cooking, stood behind long tables laden with ice tubs, grills, bottles of sauces, garnishes, breading, spices, oils, frying pans, paper plates, plastic cutlery, and more. In front of all the "makings," finished dishes in various nefarious guises were displayed for purchase and tasting.

Such disappointment – I didn't see one raw oyster. I like 'em whole, raw, iced, and un-doctored by a chef trying to play fancy.

But then I realized I didn't even see one oyster shell!

Well, I rationalized, we're out here in the middle of the country. Maybe for safety's sake the oysters were shucked at point of origin, frozen, flown in for the festival, and had to be served hot.

Having never tasted cooked oysters we continued to peruse the cook-off, trying to decide which incarnation to try first. There were sautéed oysters, braised oysters, fried oysters, BBQ'd oysters, oysters chopped up into little bits for soup, oyster chunks mixed with a jambalaya type rice concoction. Any which way you could cook oysters was sure represented at this cook-off!

And then I saw it – the elegantly carved, curved sterling silver tray sitting on four little coiled silver feet, graced with two big rounded silver handles. A large round lacy white doily had been placed on the tray.

And atop the doily? Well, at first I was quite stumped. There were two big round greyish-brownish balls placed side by side, and protruding from between them was the largest, fattest, thickest, longest asparagus spear I'd ever seen. Everyone was pointing to the tray, laughing, and taking photos. I certainly didn't get the joke; neither did my daughter. We looked at each other, clueless. But as I turned my head, I caught a glimpse of a 9 x 12 promotional poster propped up on the table – with the picture of a giant bull and the name of a local ranch.

My face turned beet red. How gullible we were! Oysters

indeed… Yes, I'd heard rumors of "testicle festivals" since moving west, but simply thought they were part and parcel of fictitious local legend. Not so, I learned that day. Each year, after bulls are routinely castrated, testicle festivals are held all over the West to share recipes and cooking tips. And the "delicacies" are affectionately dubbed "Rocky Mountain Oysters."

Mortified, my daughter and I climbed back into our car and headed for a McDonald's down the road.

But the story doesn't end there…

The following year my elderly, very proper parents came to visit. After a week or so of seeing South Dakota's sites, I drove them to Wyoming's Devil's Tower – the Devil's Tower of "Close Encounters of the Third Kind" movie fame. Before sightseeing, we stopped at a nearby diner for lunch, and slid into our booth. As a waitress approached us with menus in hand, my mother noticed a little stand-up ad at the far end of our table inviting diners to the annual local Oyster Festival that evening.

"Oh," she said to me, "how wonderful! I know you love oysters just like Dad, and all we've been eating all week is beef. We MUST go to the Oyster Festival after seeing Devil's Tower."

"Um…I don't think so, Mom," I started to say…

…as she cut me off. "I insist. It'll be a good change of pace. We haven't eaten fish or seafood all week."

At which point the waitress, upon hearing our New York accents, said "I hope you folks realize these are Rocky Mountain Oysters they'll be serving at the ranch. It's a 'testicle festival.'"

My dad's jaw hit the table.

My mother, bug-eyed, squeaked "What??"

We had Chinese food that night…

YOU KNOW YOU MOVED
TO
SOUTH DAKOTA
FROM
NEW YORK CITY...

...when "gone to seed" refers to your garden – not the way you look.

...when "throwing the bull" means you're watching a rodeo instead of spewing nonsense.

...when "climbing the ladder" indicates a barn roof needs repair rather than a corporate job promotion.

...when fishing actually involves casting a line instead of giving a gal a line.

The Woodpecker War

Throughout time, as horrible as they may have been (and I'm certainly not condoning them), many wars have had very colorful names. Think The War of the Roses, The Ragamuffin War, The Whiskey Rebellion, The Banana Wars, The War of Jenkin's Ear, The War of the Oranges, The Rum Rebellion, The Pastry War, The Pig War, and The Sheep War, to name just a few…

Well, I am currently engaged in a deadly battle: The Woodpecker War.

This war will go down in history as a fierce confrontation, greatly one-sided at two-to-one odds, with a total novice battling two experienced foes.

The battle's precursor: numerous unprovoked machine gun rounds set off one lovely bucolic morning, breaking the peace surrounding my home.

At first I thought the deafening noise was caused by riveters. Some homes here have retaining walls in their rear yards that were beginning to collapse and needed to be replaced. Sounding like the mechanical riveters gas and electricity repairmen use to break up New York City streets when underground repairs were necessary, I was certain crews had arrived to begin reconstruction of the eroding retaining walls.

Rat a tat a tatta tat tat, rat a tat a tatta tat tat, RAT A TAT A TATTA TAT TAT…and so on and so forth…

Not a very pleasant sound. And certainly not a welcome one for this homeowner who's a writer. There I was, slaving at my computer every blessed time the noise started. The carefully chosen words and phrases I was preparing in my head – ready to transfer to a page in progress – immediately just dissipated into thin air.

And this homeowner is also a meditator. Ha! Try slowly floating off into blissful silence when it feels like you're under attack!

But I consoled myself with the knowledge that the construction period would be brief and silence would once again reign supreme in a few days.

And then I saw the enemy! To be honest, this naïve city-dweller didn't at first recognize the threat. All we had to contend with when I lived in Manhattan was the occasional pigeon around open windows. You see, when you live in a tall skyscraper, your windows don't have screens because bugs don't fly high enough in the city to pose a threat to residents above, say, the tenth floor.

But every so often you'd hear a faint cooing sound when your windows were open, and sitting there on an exterior ledge would be a pigeon trying to decide whether or not to pay you an inside visit. You moved very fast to shoo it away.

So there I was in South Dakota, once again, sitting at my computer in my office in the rear of my house – RAT A TAT A TATTA TAT TAT – having just lost my trend of thought due to the latest round of riveting. The workmen, though I hadn't seen anybody from my vantage point, had already been at it for a few days. Disgusted, I paused, and looked out through the two glass doors leading onto my rear deck. There was a bird sitting there, a really big fat bird, one with which I was unfamiliar.

Lots of creatures big and small periodically show up back there: bunnies live under the deck, deer often came to visit, of course there were squirrels and an occasional raccoon, and many different kinds of birds flitted back and forth among the trees. Even saw a fox once. But I'd never seen a bird like this before. Brown toned, he was so large he could have been a crow if black.

RAT A TAT A TATTA TAT TAT…

On and off during the next few days I repeatedly saw this bird, and another just like it though the second was a lighter brown.

One day the darker bird turned its head, and even from a six foot distance, I could see that beak. Good Lord, it must have been over three inches long! I suddenly realized, "OMG, it's some kind of a woodpecker!" And then it finally dawned on me: there were no riveters fixing the retaining walls. I was being attacked by two HUGE woodpeckers!

So what do you do when there's a war? You SPY on the enemy. You gather intelligence. And you draw up a battle plan.

Over the next couple days, as soon as the attacks began I tried to locate the enemies' positions. I discovered the perpetrators had a penchant for a corner of my roof eave, and another roof eave belonging to my neighbor. Unfortunately, there was no chance of forming an alliance in this battle as my neighbor was on an extended stay out-of-town. My deck appeared to be the attackers' place of repose. Almost as if they were thumbing their beaks at me, my adversaries would periodically perch on my deck throughout the day, sunning themselves, completely unaware of the commotion they were causing when they returned to both roofs.

I did my research. Discovered woodpeckers are formidable adversaries, difficult to drive away once they find territory they covet. The best defense? A sonic blaster, tagged at over two hundred dollars. TWO HUNDRED DOLLARS!?!

My personal solution: my broom. The next few times I saw the two birds – totally frustrated, like a lunatic – I went on the attack. I lit after them waving the broom to try and scare them off.

They just waited until I went indoors and then came right back.

I contacted facebook friends for help and called my homeowners association. Two strikes there... So I returned to my research/intel phase. God bless google. Discovered woodpeckers don't like shiny, moving objects.

Well!! A battle plan formed. Maybe I could finally level the playing field here…

I headed to my local dollar store. Got ahold of the party lady. Ordered a half dozen helium-filled, shiny, bright gold Mylar balloons. Tracked down a roll of thick twine. Weapons assembled, I returned to my house and spent the next hour contemplating my plan of attack.

Three star-shaped gold reflective balloons are now tied to various locations along my deck's railing; ditto for my absent neighbor's deck. They flutter in the wind shooting piercing shiny slices of light across our properties. Yes, the helium waned after the first thirty-six hours. So I went outside and shortened the tethers. South Dakota's ever-present winds still supplied sufficient movement for the necessary light fluctuations to occur.

Though they don't land hereabouts any longer, the birds are still flying around. Tomorrow I plan to hit the dollar store again for six SILVER Mylar balloons. My neighbors must think I'm throwing one heck of an extended party.

All I'm thinkin': maybe I should buy stock in Dollar Store Incorporated just in case this turns into another Hundred Years' War…

YOU KNOW YOU MOVED TO SOUTH DAKOTA FROM NEW YORK CITY...

...when you realize a cow patty, fer sure, isn't a swirl of rich chocolate in a candy shop.

...when you're handed a ticket, not for speeding, but because it's your bill in a restaurant.

...when a washboard is your unpaved road rather than an antique artifact.

... when Wild Bill was the real thing and not some counterfeit twenty.

An Inconceivable Drive

Out here in the Wild West there's an old saying – "riding shotgun" – meaning somebody "has your back." The term originated with the sharpshooter, sitting next to the driver of a stagecoach, hired to protect passengers and cargo. As such, leaving the driver free to negotiate the trail.

Well, "something" rode shotgun with me for four days recently. The stagecoach was my car, I was its driver, and the trip was inconceivable. My tall but true tale:

The first-ever writing workshop I attended, four years ago, was held at a college in Nebraska about a two and a half hour drive from my home in South Dakota. It was a small, intimate affair, and very worthwhile.

The following year I decided to try a larger event in another state. But I found I couldn't concentrate as much on the craft of writing itself due to the crowds, logistics, social events, and the like.

So, next trip I decided to return to the cozy Nebraska program. I packed my bag, corralled my computer, filled my little 'ole Honda with gas, and quite happily hit the road.

Rapid City, South Dakota is the only major city en route to the college from my home town. All one can expect heading south to Nebraska thereafter – except for cows and corn – is the occasional truck stop/gas station along with some lovely scenery. And one pretty cool buffalo ranch… Any small South Dakota towns south of Rapid City are off-highway, and once these are passed, there is nothing at all – just a long stretch of barren road headed further south into Nebraska.

I was toodling along somewhere south of Rapid, radio on, enjoying the drive to the college when I happened to glance at my dashboard's gas meter. The indicator was at Full.

Impossible.

I regularly drive from my home town to Rapid City and use a quarter tank of gas each trip. Yet here I was a further half hour away and I appeared to still have a full tank. Surprised, I kept an eye on the indicator – it didn't budge. Figuring I should easily have under a half tank of gas by this time, I anxiously started watching for a station to fill up. Having driven this way previously, I knew how isolated the rest of the trip would be – I had no desire to run out of fuel.

Relieved, I finally spotted a station, pulled in, and – realizing something was evidently wrong with my gas indicator – gratefully started to fill my tank.

But I couldn't get any fuel into the car. The pump's nozzle kept clicking off and shutting down. I tried multiple times to fill the tank but gas would just start gushing out and run down the side of the car. Yet more than a half tank of gas had to have been used though my broken dash indicator didn't show it.

Aware how remote the remainder of the trip was, I approached the manager of the truck stop and asked for help. He said my gas tank appeared full, but managed to force close to two gallons of gas into the car. And then reassuringly said "You're only fifty miles short of your destination so you shouldn't have any problems."

With a bit of trepidation, I hopped back into the car, but thankfully made it to the college in one piece – dash gas indicator registering Full all the way.

Over the succeeding couple days, during lunch breaks, I stopped at two gas stations in town. "There's probably a methane bubble in the tank," I was told. "Comes from the high heat we've been having." But no repairs could be made over a weekend.

Before we all left for home, a number of workshop participants met for coffee the last afternoon of the conference.

One local woman, aware of the difficulties I'd been having, invited her husband along. He was in the automotive field and very graciously offered to check my car before my return drive.

We all went to a gas station. He attempted to pump gas into my tank, but fuel gushed out as before. "Your tank is full," he said.

"Can't be," I answered. "I drove from South Dakota all the way down to Nebraska, have been driving back and forth to the conference from my motel all weekend as well as to restaurants, and only refilled with less than two gallons. How can the tank be full?"

He attempted to squeeze a couple gallons into the car to assuage my fears about driving home. And I was very relieved when another Good Samaritan, a woman returning to Rapid City, said she'd tail me to make sure I didn't get stranded. And so, off we went…

I made it okay to Rapid City, waved good-bye to my protector, and again headed for a gas station. I needed to fill up to make sure I'd have enough gas for the last leg home. Sure enough, bit by bit, it was all I could do to force a gallon of gas into the tank of my car. And all the while the dash indicator continued to register Full.

Finally safely home, I decided to call Rapid's Honda dealership to check my car. Drives are long out here in the West, often with few amenities on the open roads. My car, though previously reliable, was old, and really making me nervous. So next day, I headed back to Rapid City and rolled into the dealership. I left the car to be checked, explaining the broken meter as well as the gas tank anomalies.

A couple days later a friend drove me into Rapid to retrieve the car.

The clerk looked at me strangely as she announced "We had to siphon five gallons of gas out of your tank before we could even check it. It was over-full."

"How's that possible?" I responded. "I just drove six hours between a conference and coming here, not to mention driving to restaurants and my motel while I was gone. That's a total of over 360 miles. So how could my gas tank be full – with five extra gallons yet?"

"Can't answer that. There was no methane bubble, and except for the broken indicator dial everything is working fine.

"And by the way," she added, "when we finished the repairs we reinserted the five extra gallons of gas we removed. So right now you have a full tank PLUS the five gallons you forced into the car at your various stops. Gonna be a while before you'll need to gas up again…"

"But I still don't understand how after all that mileage I had a full tank…"

And the clerk smiled mysteriously and said "Someone, or better yet something, was sure 'riding shotgun' for you to make certain you were protected – that you'd make that writing conference and not get stranded…"

YOU KNOW YOU MOVED TO SOUTH DAKOTA FROM NEW YORK CITY...

…when John Deere isn't a break-up letter.

…when a pickup has four wheels instead of two legs.

…when dough tends more to cookies and pies than dollars and cents.

…when "silent night" is every night – not just a Christmas carol.

Frosty Fairytale

:
Every flyer's nightmare: my luggage had been lost. So three days into my ten day overseas island trip, with no valise in sight, I finally located a department store for some emergency replacement clothing.

My airline kept assuring me my valise would be found. But by trip's end, my luggage still hadn't materialized. Now the issue was how to transport my newly purchased clothes and souvenirs home sans a suitcase.

A second trip to the local island department store was an eye-opener. Used to "big box" stores in the United States that discounted luggage prices, I had sticker shock when checking out the small ultra-expensive selection available. Sure, there was a flea market in the area that might have helped, but my flight left before its next scheduled date. What to do? Ship cardboard boxes home? But then I'd have a customs hassle…

While in the store I noticed two "garment-bags" on sale – the thin plastic zip-sacks generally used to protect clothes hung in a car or dumped in its trunk. They were probably on sale because of their really outlandish numbing color – a screaming, shocking, electric neon blue. In desperation I purchased these, and my airline – cognizant of my missing valise – courteously let me stash the two bags in the plane's overhead cabin bins on my return flight. Their fabric just wasn't strong enough to withstand the rigors of the plane's luggage hold.

I had planned a "layover" in New York on my way home to South Dakota to visit my two children who still lived in

Manhattan. My son picked me up at John F. Kennedy airport. Upon spotting the two hideously colored blue garment bags slung over each of my arms, aghast, he sputtered, "Mom – how *could* you?!?"

WINTER, FOLLOWING YEAR:

Fast forward to the following winter. My son decides to visit me in South Dakota for the Christmas holidays to try the skiing, snow-boarding, and snow-mobile trails located near my house; taste the special seasonal menus at local restaurants and inns; enjoy all our many varied festivities. We also scheduled a couple days' general sightseeing together – it would be lovely seeing the area under a blanket of newly fallen snow.

I packed my clothes while he was out on his last ski run. Since we were driving, I decided to use one of the two screaming, shocking, electric neon blue garment bags from my previous trip. Ugly as it was, it was perfect for this little jaunt. Stuffed with warm clothing due to one of South Dakota's really cold Canadian arctic snaps, I threw it into the trunk of my car and closed the lid. A couple hours later, after depositing his duffel bag onto my car's back seat, the two of us embarked upon our journey.

It was bitterly cold as we left, and became colder still as the day wore on. When we reached our destination for the evening my car radio informed us that, factoring in wind chill, it was twelve below. Yet the tourist town we were visiting was jammed with holiday revelers shopping, dining, sightseeing – locals as well as visitors. We couldn't find a parking space in our hotel's lot – it was packed solid. We oh-so-slowly inched our way round and round hoping someone would vacate a space, to no avail. To boot, there was gridlock at the hotel's front door with arriving and departing guests and diners.

My son, who was driving, finally suggested he try to find parking off-property. To save me a longish walk in the bitter cold, I exited the car where we were at that point, about two blocks from the hotel. I took my garment bag from the trunk.

He'd carry his duffel bag – still stashed on the rear seat of the car – from wherever he happened to find street parking. Our plan, after we each checked into our respective rooms: we'd meet for dinner in the hotel's lobby restaurant in an hour's time.

I started trudging towards the hotel, garment bag in tow. While walking I started hearing faint "crinkle-crinkle" sounds, but figured they were due to my boots scrunching the packed snow underfoot.

Upon entering the hotel's lovely reception area I proceeded to the check-in desk. I was shocked when one of the two attendants shot me a withering look. "What on earth have I done to deserve that?" I thought. And then he disappeared…

Room assigned. Twenty minutes later I heard an unexpected knock on my door. It was my son suggesting we immediately go down for dinner in the hotel's lobby. A line had begun forming at the restaurant – seems a number of people didn't want to brave the bitter cold or lose their coveted parking spots!

I was so surprised to see him standing there in the hall, holding his duffel bag. He evidently hadn't gone to his room yet. How did he know where to find me? "Reception" hadn't phoned to inform me someone was asking for my room number; checking if I was expecting a guest. Did they just divulge room numbers to anyone who asked? Not good security at all! And my son hadn't called on his cell. Concerned, I asked how he managed to discover which room I was in.

"Easy," he answered. "I saw your trail."

"My what??"

'Yup," he laughed, "your trail. Couldn't be missed. I just followed it straight to your room. Kinda like in the fairytale 'Hansel and Gretel.'"

Had he lost his mind?

"Mom," he explained, "there's only one outlandish color like that in the entire world. The instant I saw it I remembered the screaming, shocking, electric neon blue from JFK airport when I picked you up last year. Only *you* could be associated with that color! So I followed the trail – and of course it led me straight to your room."

"Catch me up, please. I'm a little confused here…"

"Mom, I spent my four years of college in New Hampshire. We often had real frigid weather like today's temps. When it's this cold, thin plastic freezes. Your garment bag was in the trunk of the car all day – it froze! It evidently started to crack and shred as you walked towards the hotel because you left a couple blocks' trail – strewn along the stark white snowy sidewalk – of tiny frozen screaming, shocking, electric neon blue plastic flakes. I followed them straight to your door!"

I looked at him, unconvinced.

He waved his arm. "Take a look down the hall…"

I poked my head out of my room and looked down the hotel's hallway. Sure enough, sitting atop the pastel lemon yellow and light green flowered carpet, there was an unmistakable long snaking line of screaming, shocking, electric neon blue flakes.

I opened my closet door. Barely visible, there were spider-web lines meandering all over the garment bag's shocking blue fabric. And while its top was still somewhat whole – so that I didn't realize it was disintegrating during my walk or when I hung it up – the entire bottom was now missing tiny pieces here, there, everywhere. A small pile of flakes had even begun accruing on the floor of the closet.

Suddenly the "crinkle" sounds I'd heard when walking made sense – the frozen plastic fabric had been cracking!

After a good laugh we headed to the hotel lobby for dinner, retracing our steps via the blue Hansel and Gretel trail. The disapproving reception attendant, meanwhile, had reappeared armed with a vacuum, broom, and dustpan. I apologized profusely for the mess. Wearily he commented "You're not the first today, and you won't be the last."

I looked outside the hotel's front door. Yes, down the block there stretched a long line of tiny, brilliant, neon blue specks highlighted against the white snow, shining in the glow of lit

Christmas decorations,.

My son laughed. "See – 'Hansel and Gretel!' All I had to do was follow your trail."

Hansel and Gretel indeed. To this day, as winter approaches, every time I spy a candy-decorated gingerbread house – in a bakery window or restaurant, on a do-it-yourself baking kit, or in a child's picture book – I recall the iconic fairytale. And then I chuckle at the memory of my son following my Hansel and Gretel screaming, shocking, electric neon blue frozen confetti trail to my room.

CONCLUSION:

Great visit with my son, but alas, the garment bag was a total loss – it just kept shredding!

Déjà vu: second winter trip with no luggage for my homeward journey.

Hmmmm… Must be that wicked witch…

YOU KNOW YOU MOVED TO SOUTH DAKOTA FROM NEW YORK CITY...

...when you discover folks don't just hunt for game, they also hunt for asparagus.

...when "dear season" doesn't refer to Valentine's Day. Yup, hunting again.

...when "the great white way" is the expanse of snow in your driveway rather than the bright lights of Broadway.

...when a guy's swollen-looking cheek isn't a toothache – he's chewin' tobacco!

Fugitive

Shades of Butch Cassidy and the Sundance Kid out here in the West – I was a fugitive!!

A little back-story first…

I'm actually a pretty responsible, fairly level-headed, law-abiding citizen (if I do say so myself). Although you wouldn't know it since I left New York City for South Dakota. As an adult, in all the years I lived back east, there were only two run-ins with the law – and only one of these actually had to do with something I did (and it was kinda justified)…

Run-in #1: our house was robbed, so of course we called the police.

Run-in #2: my son's college graduation up in New Hampshire, when construction delays made us late for the ceremony – I received my very-first-ever speeding ticket after decades of driving.

But out here in South Dakota, during the first few years I relocated, I seemed to get into scrapes with the law all the time. Innocently, yes, but nevertheless still an issue.

So I'd already messed with the military police and had a to-do in Spearfish when I didn't realize a van was a police car. Then, after our tornado, I unknowingly insulted a sheriff.

Scenario four occurred late one dark night up at the Heritage Museum in town. After living in a busy suburb, and then directly in Manhattan for a number of years, I wasn't used to seeing beautiful starry nights. Between the light pollution and multitudinous skyscrapers, sky viewing was an impossible quest.

But out here in South Dakota I found a new passion. Armed with seasonal constellation charts, I'd search out a perfect viewing spot and muse away, sometimes meditating afterwards. There were a couple spots in town that worked on nights I didn't feel like driving about. I loved higher locations, and so occasionally would park in the lot on the hill of the silent, shuttered Heritage Museum.

One such night I pulled in and shut my car's motor and lights. Busy trying to align my location to the night sky on my chart, a loud thump suddenly shocked me. There, having jumped onto the front hood of my car, sat a big black cat staring at me through my windshield, gold eyes boring into me. I laughed – but should have taken its presence as a warning.

Eventually, once the kitty departed, I closed my eyes and went into meditation. And then suddenly there was raucous rapping on my window. I opened my eyes, and sure enough, there stood a policeman – he had some questions for me.

It seems a local resident, working a late shift, regularly passed by the Heritage on his drive home and had seen my car in the lot a number of times. He alerted the police – thought I was "casing" the museum prior to a break-in.

So ended my in-town night rambles…

But my weirdest run-in with the law was yet to come.

It was a Thursday, the day SD's peripatetic Motor Vehicles Bureau is in Spearfish, my home town. I dutifully reported to renew my driver's license. This was super important as I was leaving early the following Tuesday morning on a business trip during which I'd be doing quite a bit of driving.

After filling out the necessary forms and waiting a few minutes, it was my turn for the eye exam, photo and whatever else clerks review on their computers. All run of the mill – or so I thought.

The woman doing my background check suddenly said, "I can't renew this."

I was stunned. "Why ever not?"

Her answer: "You're 'wanted' in two states."

"I'm WHAT??"

"You're 'wanted' in two states – Wyoming and South Dakota."

Shaking my head, "There has to be a mistake. I've had no tickets, no car problems. Have no outstanding debts. Can you please check again?" And I explained how important it was for me to obtain my new license that day.

"Nothing I can do," she said. "I already checked twice. You're 'wanted.'"

And so began a nightmarish trip through the red tape of bureaucracy – multitudinous phone calls trying to discover why I was a fugitive. Calls to three states, no less – SD, WY, and NY – with only two hours that Thursday afternoon before everything closed down, and Friday, to solve the problem. And if solved, I'd first have to visit a neighboring town the following Monday, my only day remaining before leaving – because that's where the Motor Vehicles Bureau would be stationed on their rotating schedule.

Talk about stress!!

After endless calls playing Sherlock Holmes, around 4:30pm Friday afternoon I finally discovered why my new license had been withheld: subsequent to a car accident a few years prior my insurance company neglected to file a closing statement.

I was furious – all this lost time and angst because of an oversight. Not to mention having a "wanted" status on record…

After much haranguing and threatening on the phone – I needed a written statement from the company that everything had been resolved – we devised a plan. Via overnight express, they'd get a signed letter to me Monday morning to take to the DMV in the next town that afternoon, so I could fly out with my new driver's license Tuesday morning. An insurance employee would have to work overtime Friday evening to draft the letter – their problem, not mine. They owed me!

Woe the day I related this story – my two children will never let me live it down. Even now, years later, when I enter a room after not seeing them for a while, one will look at the other, eyes twinkling, and from a few feet away I can lip-read the whispered refrain:

"Here comes the fugitive, a Western legend…"

And then the other grins and answers "Yup, 'wanted' in two states…"

YOU KNOW YOU MOVED TO SOUTH DAKOTA FROM NEW YORK CITY...

...when a mouse runs free in a barn instead of being connected to a computer.

...when ice fishing has nothing to do with trying to spear your strawberry in a frozen daiquiri.

...when a barb isn't a sharp retort – it's a twisted piece of wire on a fence.

Icing on the Cake

So I've loved living out here in South Dakota. The state definitely had what I'd been searching for when I decided to move from New York City: fresh air, lots of sunshine, beautiful scenery, good water, no crowds, no traffic, a slower pace, little crime, decent weather, pleasant people. With a genuine Western, cowboyish, laid-back, slower atmosphere thrown into the mix...

Yes, the famed Marlboro Man on all those billboard advertisements really does exist!

Not that life was so bad back in New York. At the time I loved the hectic pace, the theater, the museums and galleries, strolls along the Hudson River's bank, Central Park, all the ethnic restaurants and funky shops, the great variety of movies, music and programs available. It's just that each area has its own special beauty, characteristics, and personality, and I was ready for a change.

The only issue when I first moved: I had trouble sleeping out here in the West. When I mentioned this to new friends, they always attributed the problem to the fact that it's so quiet at night compared to what I was used to.

But that wasn't the reason. This was the very first time in years where I wasn't sleeping at night with an activated burglar alarm or a front-desk concierge to ward off any unwanted visitors. Took me a long time to get used to this. Especially because I live in a ground level house. And though I eventually became comfortable enough to sleep soundly at night, I still can't do so with open windows – which to an easterner is an invitation to intruders.

It literally blows my mind that people out here not only sleep with open windows – they actually go to bed at night without locking their doors.

And leave their houses unlocked during the day...

And leave their car's motor running when they make a quick stop at a shop or the post office!

The differences between the Northeast and West are many – often surprising and sometimes amusing. Take shopping, for example. When I first moved here and told friends back east there were exactly *two* large, department-store-anchored Malls in the entire *state*, they were absolutely incredulous. Yes, other South Dakota shopping areas may have considered themselves as such, but they basically were strip malls – not actual legit, *large* malls with a capital M.

And so it was with tremendous pleasure and much anticipation that I awaited the completion of Rapid City's second Mall a few years ago – a mall worthy of a capital M. Yes, I loved all that I'd moved here for, but a little gentrification wasn't SUCH a terrible thing...no? Kinda like a little icing on the cake??

Surprisingly, a year or so before groundbreaking began on the new Mall, a couple sushi places had even opened in Rapid. And then Starbucks made an appearance.

Oh my...

After completion, I decided to drive into Rapid to check out the newly opened Mall. The recent recession had slowed some of its development but, yes, it was legit – an actual mall with a capital M. Most of the anchors were familiar, but some fresh faces – a bunch of smaller establishments – had taken root. I thoroughly enjoyed walking around and browsing through some of the stores.

And then it was time for dinner...

I headed over to my favorite sushi place. Did justice to a couple rolls. Then decided I was thirsty, hopped into my car, and made a stop on the way home. Sitting in the outdoor café area, coffee cup in hand, I chuckled, picked up my cell phone and called my daughter back in New York City.

"Don't laugh," I announced, "we have arrived!! Cute, little Rapid City is definitely on the map!"

"What in the world are you talking about?" she asked.

"Well," I said, "I never thought I'd see the day. But here I am, after being a South Dakota resident all these years, drinking coffee in the outdoor café of a Starbucks after a delicious sushi dinner and a shopping spree at TJ Maxx. All right here in Rapid City – Starbucks, sushi, and TJ Maxx – who wudda thought! It's absolutely amazing. We have definitely 'arrived.' The outside world has discovered us!"

Truly, it's been most interesting to watch South Dakota spread its wings a little bit over the twenty years I've lived in Spearfish. Now that doesn't mean I want this special little corner of the globe to grow much larger or more commercial – I love it as is. It's just been fun gaining a couple more choices.

However, now that the outside world has found *us*, how about us having the opportunity to learn a bit more about the outside world? We all live on a shrinking planet today and everything is inextricably intertwined. Change is inevitable.

So how about a foreign film/indie movie theater, please? There's more to life than fictitious superheroes and there's plenty of room at the Mall.

Now that would *really* be the "icing on the cake."

As for me, I'll take a latte to go with that cake…

Wait, scratch the cake – I'll have a donut instead!

Epilogue

Two roads diverged in a wood, and I –
I took the one less traveled by,
And that has made all the difference.
                    – Robert Frost, *The Road Not Taken*

And what an absolute delight to discover the road less traveled
is your own personal, perfect fit.

So much so that I never even think of "the road not taken…"

Here's to the discoveries, challenges, and pleasures of
the journey. May everyone's choices prove enjoyable and
enlightening…

About the Author

Marsha Warren Mittman's poetry, short stories, and essays have been widely published in American, British, German, and Australian literary journals, magazines, and anthologies, including six *Chicken Soup for the Soul* tales. She's authored three poetry chapbooks: *Patriarchal Chronicles – Women's Worldwide Tears* was accepted for publication, and select poems are currently being crafted into a staged "readers' theater" production; *Message from a Goldfish – A Guide to Awareness* was used in meditation programs in a dozen states. Mittman's received numerous poetry and prose distinctions in the U.S. and Ireland, and was recently awarded a writing residency at the Fairhope Center for the Writing Arts in Alabama. An avid traveler, she's visited over 125 countries/islands on six continents, and forty-six American states. For the past twenty years South Dakota's beautiful Black Hills have been home base.

Made in the USA
Monee, IL
26 January 2020

20885090R00125